Natural Genius

of related interest

The Complete Guide to Asperger's Syndrome
Tony Attwood
ISBN-13: 978 1 84310 495 7   ISBN-10: 1 84310 495 4

Asperger's Syndrome
A Guide for Parents and Professionals
Tony Attwood
Foreword by Lorna Wing
ISBN-13: 978 1 85302 577 8   ISBN-10: 1 85302 577 1

Different Minds
Gifted Children with AD/HD, Asperger Syndrome,
and Other Learning Deficits
Deirdre V. Lovecky
ISBN-13: 978 1 85302 964 6   ISBN-10: 1 85302 964 5

Pretending to be Normal
Living with Asperger's Syndrome
Liane Holliday Willey
Foreword by Tony Attwood
ISBN-13: 978 1 85302 749 9   ISBN-10: 1 85302 749 9

Freaks, Geeks and Asperger Syndrome
A User Guide to Adolescence
Luke Jackson
Foreword by Tony Attwood
ISBN-13: 978 1 84310 098 0   ISBN-10: 1 84310 098 3

Asperger's Syndrome and High Achievement
Some Very Remarkable People
Ioan James
ISBN-13: 978 1 84310 388 2   ISBN-10: 1 84310 388 5

Elijah's Cup
A Family's Journey into the Community and Culture of High-functioning
Autism and Asperger's Syndrome (Revised edition)
Valerie Paradi
ISBN-13: 978 1 84310 802 3   ISBN-10: 1 84310 802 X

Finding a Different Kind of Normal
Misadventures with Asperger Syndrome
Jeanette Purkis
Foreword by Donna Williams
ISBN-13: 978 1 84310 416 2   ISBN-10: 1 84310 416 4

Natural Genius

The Gifts of Asperger's Syndrome

Susan Rubinyi

Jessica Kingsley Publishers
London and Philadelphia

First published in 2007
by Jessica Kingsley Publishers
116 Pentonville Road
London N1 9JB, UK
and
400 Market Street, Suite 400
Philadelphia, PA 19106, USA

www.jkp.com

Library of Congress Cataloging in Publication Data
Rubinyi, Susan, 1946-
 Natural genius : the gifts of Asperger's syndrome / Susan Rubinyi.
  p. cm.
 ISBN-13: 978-1-84310-784-2 (alk. paper)
 ISBN-10: 1-84310-784-8 (alk. paper)
 1. Rubinyi, Susan, 1946- 2. Parents of autistic children--United States--Biography. 3.
Asperger's syndrome in children. I. Title.
 RJ506.A9R83 2006
 618.92'858820092--dc22
 [B]

2006029531

British Library Cataloguing in Publication Data
A CIP catalogue record for this book is available from the British Library

ISBN-13: 978 1 84310 784 2
ISBN-10: 1 84310 784 8

Printed and Bound in the United States by Thomson-Shore, Inc.

*To my mother, Erland, Ben, Roby, and Andy
who helped excavate through the seemingly
impenetrable rock of Asperger's Syndrome
to uncover the hidden gold within*

Contents

Chapter One

My journey begins and ends at the ocean. As a child in Southern California, I had a recurrent dream of the ocean. My parents' house was located in the mountains with only a distant view of the water. In my dream, however, the ocean appears right outside of our house, waves luminous in the early morning light. A newly born beach, covered with glistening shells beckons. I rush outside, mind and body filled with wonder and expectation. I sense I may wander endlessly into this expansive landscape, no limits to the directions my explorations may take.

I have returned to this dream/vision many times as I have navigated the often alien landscape of developing a positive approach for raising a child with Asperger's Syndrome. My journey has pushed me to the extreme limits of my creative potential, at times involving extreme pain, at times, immense joy. At the beginning, in 1986 when Ben was born, I didn't know the name of the territory I was journeying through and, in a way, this has proved to be an advantage in creating a strength-based approach.

Foremost in my mind was to try to design a method which would allow my child's gifts and potential the widest possible landscape in which to develop, I hoped free from some of the constraints I felt had blocked parts of my own development. Only later in the journey did I discover I was really on a second journey as well, one of self-discovery, for which my child's unique make-up would prove to be a catalyst for exploring issues critical to my own continued growth.

My journey has involved returning emotionally and physically to the place of my birth, Los Angeles, after a voluntary exile of 35 years. The ocean, as in my childhood, provides an immense source of solace as I begin to explore both the pain and enjoyment I experienced growing up here. Years before Ben's birth, I was planting the seeds for a method based on the child's gifts and strengths.

Two of my strongest childhood interests have provided invaluable tools for raising a child with Asperger's Syndrome—science fiction and foreign languages and cultures. Both of these interests would stretch my imagination far past previous limits of the possible. So, when I finally encountered Asperger's Syndrome, I was already intimately familiar with far more alien perspectives.

It's no accident that science fiction is often the "literature of choice" for people with Asperger's Syndrome. Many aspects of science fiction, which I began reading at age nine, have helped me immensely to understand and navigate my way through the universe of a person with Asperger's Syndrome. Fortunately, no one ever told me, as was common in the 1950s, that "girls don't read science fiction."

Readers of SF quickly become conversant with concepts such as parallel universes and alternative dimensions where changing a single premise can totally change the course of history. In a classic Ray Bradbury story, a time traveler visiting a primordial forest accidentally steps off the path, drastically altering evolutionary history. In the Asperger's universe as well, what at first sight may appear as chaotic and incomprehensible from a neurotypical point of view, makes logical sense within the child's mind when traced back to the original premise. One example of this occurred with Ben even before the Asperger's diagnosis appeared in the *Diagnostic and Statistical Manual of Mental Disorders – Fourth Edition* (DSM-IV).

In the first grade, the principal told him:

"Go back to your class."

Curious to see what he would do, she watched him from a distance. Rather than returning to his classroom as she expected, he made his way to the gym.

"And he was completely right," she told me, "because that's exactly where his class was at the time."

A less perceptive principal might have criticized Ben for not following directions but he was actually following his internal logical system. Here, his Asperger's quality of interpreting things literally, "go rejoin your class," plus his photographic memory served as strengths rather than deficits.

In the years that have followed, I've used this example of "parallel universes and alternative dimensions" as a guide to tracing the internal logic of Ben's actions and thought processes back to their original premises, enabling me and others to deal with them more effectively.

Another lesson I've learned from science fiction is to recognize alternative modes of communication—i.e., aliens who communicate through music, telepathy, telekinesis—as well as aliens whose concept of time may differ radically from ours. I've realized that Ben's emotions sometimes exist in a time warp. He may express intense sadness, anger, excitement with great immediacy but, as I investigate further, he is actually dealing with emotions related to events that happened a decade ago, with a sense of present intensity. Defining where we are in his "time warp," as well as his mode of communication, assumes great importance in understanding how to proceed forward.

Science fiction has also shown me the consequences of genetic variation—experiments into the nature of intelligence can have unforeseen emotional and intellectual consequences. Who is to say what we may eventually learn about the genetic causes and potentially positive implications of Asperger's Syndrome? Science fiction taught me that one must always look beneath the surface—that a monstrous external appearance may house a sensitive intelligent consciousness; that what one person sees as hideous and disturbing can appear beautiful from another perspective. The literature greatly broadened my definition of the possible, widening my understanding of how the word "normal" can limit both tolerance and the imagination.

My attraction to science fiction had another, sadder side to it as well—an element of "escape from" as well as "escape to." A part of me had always felt like an alien growing up in Los Angeles. Though I am the parent of rather than a person with Asperger's Syndrome, I live close enough to the border (on what Dr. Tony Attwood calls the "gifted eccentric side") to understand much of the territory.

I have some idea of what it feels like to experience a strong discontinuity between whom one is inside and the surrounding environment, to feel like a "stranger in a strange land." In French, interestingly enough, the word for "stranger" (*étranger*) is also used in science fiction for "alien." Throughout my childhood, I felt as though I had somehow been transported to an alien planet whose overwhelming sensory input assaulted me, whose social customs remained a mystery to me, whose language didn't possess the vocabulary to express my thoughts and emotions. I saw myself as an exile who would one day go in search of her native land.

In addition to my love of science fiction, my background in music would also prove invaluable to raising a child with Asperger's Syndrome. From my father, a professional pianist, I inherited a gift for music, which would later pass down to Ben in even stronger form, partly because of the syndrome. My own musical training helped me recognize Ben's perfect pitch early on, his ability to reproduce exact vocal and instrumental nuances.

When Ben was a few years old, he was able to pick out Beethoven's "Ode to Joy" on the piano. Resolving not to repeat my own ambivalent experience of not having a right to choose my own instrument, I didn't try to channel him into an instrument of *my* choice. I vowed to let his musical ability develop in its own way so that music could always remain a joy to him.

Ben's gift would prove to have its own problematic side, that we would later understand was augmented by his Asperger's Syndrome. Someone with such an acute ear can also have hyperacuity, an over-sensitivity to sound, at times verging on the painful. His hyperacuity would make conventional classroom education extremely difficult as would his highly unusual learning style.

My own early educational experience helped sensitize me to recognize different learning styles, which sometimes run contrary to current educational theory. Reading in the 1950s was taught using a primarily visual method, the Dick and Jane readers. As an auditory learner, I was faced with daily torture and frustration, knowing inside I was perfectly capable of acquiring this new skill but needing to get there by a different route.

My intellectual potential ignored, I was placed in a lower reading group where I knew I didn't belong. Angry, I performed one of my few acts of "civil disobedience" by deliberately talking during the higher reading group. When I got into trouble, I quickly became a "suffer in silence" type who was a model of good behavior, somehow developing my own method for learning to read. Learning how to develop alternative approaches when the conventional didn't work would also stand me in good stead with Ben.

By the time I reached secondary school, I had developed a rich inner intellectual life while presenting a shy outward façade. My intelligence and creative ability weren't recognized for three years by my teachers, though they were by my peers.

"You really belong in the gifted classes," one girl told me. "People don't realize how smart you are because you're so quiet."

My educational experience, as with my science fiction reading, helped me realize intelligence and giftedness can take many different forms. Parents must be committed to looking beneath the surface, initially going on faith in the child's potential (this would again prove to be the case with my Asperger's son). I also learned one must search out environments and resources that will nourish the child's growth. One of these, for me, was the summer Idyllwild School of Music and the Arts, located in the mountains, combining music, nature, and eventually travel.

Almost immediately, I had finally found an environment where I no longer felt like an alien. At last, for two weeks of the year, I was among kindred spirits, intelligent, artistic, who spoke the same language. For the first time in my life, I could make friends easily (a process that continued to baffle me in school). I discovered a prototype for a nurturing environment, a model to which I would refer back as I sought to locate and/or create resources for Ben.

During the school year, in a conventional environment, my initial timidity and lack of understanding of "normal" teenage social customs often led to painful feelings of social isolation. These feelings, for a person with Asperger's Syndrome like Ben, are multiplied a thousand-fold. Though the absolute honesty of Asperger's Syndrome can sometimes be difficult to take, I prefer it to the betrayal, the subterfuge I experienced at times, inflicted on me by so-called "normal" teenagers.

For years, I buried my pain of being rejected for being different, only to have it resurface decades later as Ben's difficulties with social interactions began. I realized that if my difference from social norms lay continents away, Ben's lay light years away. One unexpected positive, however, was that I began to see difference as a potential asset with its own creative possibilities. Secondary school, though difficult, provided me with another essential tool for raising Ben—my discovery of foreign languages and cultures.

Even before I began to study French, the idea of learning another language excited me. The image of a bubble around my head came to me—that by learning a language, I would be immersed in a whole new way of thinking and feeling, a vastly different world view. Fortunately my highly gifted teacher utilized an auditory approach and I soon began to study Russian as well.

For the first time, I experienced not only being good at something and having my ability recognized but also deeply enjoying what I was doing. Somehow, when I began speaking another language I was able to enter fully into the experience, assume a different perspective; these too were skills that would prove essential for raising Ben.

I found that emotions that remained inaccessible to me in English could easily be expressed in French. I discovered that each language seemed to emphasize its own part of the emotional spectrum. Though I have since done interpreting and translating, I see these as only rough approximations of what one experiences in the original language.

With the immersion method where no English was used (we even said the Pledge of Allegiance in Russian!) our teacher taught us not only language but culture as well. Through music, poetry, cuisine, we entered a rich and complex world. I would later use these total immersion techniques in my own teaching and in raising Ben bilingually.

Towards the end of high school, however, I was beginning to develop a few close friendships among other intellectually inclined students. One of these was with Greg, a fellow devotee of Baroque music, who later would become Ben's father. The more I got to know Greg, the more I felt I had finally met someone who spoke the same language. Little did I suspect that a part of this language may well have been Asperger's Syndrome, as we would discover after Ben's birth over two decades later.

After graduation, I left Los Angeles for the University of California, Berkeley, vowing never to return to the city of my birth for anything longer than a vacation. I kept this vow for 35 years. Yet the pain of my school experience was only dormant, not extinct, and would resurface years later after the birth of my Asperger's Syndrome child.

My undergraduate education at Berkeley began the same year as the Free Speech Movement—initially a radical questioning of the political, it ultimately led to the Anti-Vietnam War protests, the sexual revolution, feminism, and the ecological movement. My years at Berkeley widened my perspective on the possible including alternate approaches and tolerance of difference. Later, one of my eventual forays into this new territory of expanding human potential would involve co-editing one of the first feminist science fiction anthologies, *Aurora: Beyond Equality*, published by Fawcett Gold Medal, Greenwich, CT, in 1976.

I credit Berkeley not only with broadening my understanding of different possibilities and questioning conventional approaches but also with empowering me with the courage to struggle with bureaucracies as I would need to do for searching out or creating resources for a child with Asperger's Syndrome. This struggle, unfortunately, continues to this day and part of what I see as my mission in writing this book is not only to help families but also, I hope, to encourage those in education and mental health to see the positive potential of people with Asperger's Syndrome rather than focusing primarily on the challenges.

I spent my Junior Year in France, which enabled me to acquire a level of proficiency that would one day have the additional benefit of enabling me to raise a child bilingually. For the first time in my life, I experienced what total immersion in another culture truly meant, where every aspect of life took place in a different language. Ordering breakfast, visiting museums, asking for directions required me quickly to expand my level of comprehension of native speakers who didn't slow down to pedagogical levels.

I discovered that much of my vocabulary was literary, not corresponding to everyday objects and interactions. Though I knew the literal meanings of many words, the linguistic nuances often escaped me. Once, for example, when the lights went out where I was staying, I was told: "Vous avez fait sauté les plombs," which, literally translated means: "You made the leads jump." Later I figured out I'd blown the fuses.

Years later, this linguistic confusion would help me understand an Asperger's Syndrome person's focus on literal rather than figurative meanings—what neurotypicals consider a deficit yet themselves experience when learning a second language.

Another aspect of my time in France closely related to the Asperger's experience involved frequently colliding with invisible walls of alien social rules. These were never explained to me in advance yet my actions were censured after the fact. The first night I arrived at the family where I would spend a year, they asked me detailed questions about my parents' professions. Taking an American point of view, I interpreted this as friendly interest. As it turned out, however, they were trying to ascertain where to place me in their social class system, an institution as alien to me as I must have seemed to them.

Fortunately, I met another, less class-conscious, family who took a genuine interest in me as a person, welcoming someone from another culture into their own. In a relaxed, friendly atmosphere of tolerance,

I acquired near-native fluency in French. Later, I could apply this experience to Ben, both in encouraging his bilingualism and in helping nurture the development of the gifted side of his Asperger's Syndrome, focusing on his positive potential rather than solely his challenges. My experience abroad helped me develop compassion not only for what foreign students go through in our country but also, multiplied a thousand-fold, what a person with Asperger's Syndrome experiences on a daily basis.

By the time Ben was born, 17 years after Greg and I got married, I had already lived in France, Spain, Hawaii, and the Pacific Northwest and worked as a writer, editor, administrator, and teacher. Little did I realize that, with Ben's birth, I would be setting forth on a journey, which would take me to the utmost limits of my potential as I learned to deal with the gifts and challenges of a child with Asperger's Syndrome.

Though I was entering unknown territory, early in my pregnancy I had already made what would prove to be a crucial decision in ways I didn't imagine—the decision to raise Ben bilingually.

Chapter Two

Visiting Ashland during my pregnancy, my friend suggested the possibility of bilingualism.

"With all the languages you speak, have you ever considered raising your child bilingually?" she asked. "If so, I have a book I can recommend."

I got a copy of *Bringing Up Baby Bilingual* by Jane Merrill, published by Facts on File Inc., NY, in 1989, and quickly immersed myself in it. I learned that as long as children are exposed to a second language by age 11, they can learn to speak it fluently with a native accent. After age 11, it's as if a door closes in the brain, making it much harder to reach a native level of proficiency.

I vowed to give our baby an opportunity I hadn't had since my first exposure to French wasn't until age 12. My years of teaching college French had also shown me how difficult it was for older students to pick up a second language. I began searching out French children's books and, even before Ben was born, started reading out loud in French. Since I was still teaching French and Russian during my pregnancy, Ben also had four months' exposure to both *in utero*.

Following the total immersion approach advocated in *Bringing Up Baby Bilingual*, I vowed to speak nothing but French to him from the moment he was born. What I hadn't anticipated was the exhaustion of an 18-hour labor. Somehow, I had believed that if I just performed my La Maze breathing properly, I wouldn't experience any pain. I soon realized, however, that the word "intense" was a euphemism for "painful." I also wasn't prepared for my first look at the baby who, for nine months, had shared my body space.

In his clear, lucid eyes, I could immediately sense a very powerful energy, hidden from me until the moment of birth. His gaze was so strong I couldn't meet it for four days. Then, though still exhausted from the rigors of childbirth, I began to speak French to him, which I would continue to do exclusively until he was 12. At the beginning, I had to proceed totally on faith, that somehow, when Ben began to speak, the words spoken to me would come out in French.

We followed the "one face, one language" model of bilingualism, with me speaking French, Greg speaking English. Ben's developmental milestones were perfectly normal during his first year. He began walking around 11 months, talking about the same time. We're still not sure if his first word was "disc/record" in French or "this" in English. He quickly became fluent in both languages.

Though I had no inkling at the beginning that the bright little baby I was raising bilingually would also turn out to have Asperger's Syndrome, I am now convinced that the choice of bilingualism has helped develop alternative pathways in his brain that would otherwise not have been utilized. Even a neurotypical bilingual exhibits much greater ability than a monolingual in learning third, fourth, fifth languages.

I see multiple additional advantages of bilingualism for a person with Asperger's Syndrome, who has challenges with flexibility and understanding the existence of different perspectives. Merely the fact that there are two different ways to describe the same object, concept, in each language, enlarges the perception of the possible. Since a bilingual learns culture as well as language, the child sees alternative ways of approaching multiple areas of life (eating, recreation, transportation etc.). What is customary in one culture is not necessarily customary in another: for example, people eat multi-course meals in France at different hours from American meals, there are other definitions of what are acceptable conversational topics. Understanding cultural variations can provide a model for an Asperger's Syndrome person to understand the neurotypical world and vice versa.

I believe, because of bilingualism, Ben's brain had a chance to partly rewire itself even before his Asperger's Syndrome became manifest. I once saw a very moving documentary about a violinist with epilepsy. When all other measures failed, she decided to risk an operation even though the part of the brain to be operated on also controlled musical ability. No one could predict whether or not she would still be able to perform. In the most moving scene in the film, the post-operative woman picks up a violin and begins to play a Bach unaccompanied sonata. The neurologist concludes her brain had indeed rewired itself.

I have often been told by native speakers of both languages how articulate Ben is, often much more so than someone without Asperger's Syndrome. I would guess this may not have been the case had he not have been raised bilingually. His extraordinary gift of being able to reproduce verbal and musical nuances exactly gives his language an expressiveness and multi-tonality often said to be lacking in monolingual Asperger's people.

I have heard bilingualism blamed so often as the cause of every conceivable emotional difficulty a child may develop that I feel it's time to correct the balance and point out the positive aspects. Raising any child bilingually requires a great deal of commitment and perseverance on the part of a parent and is not made easier by uninformed criticism ("If you'd stop speaking French to him, he'd behave normally").

The fact that Ben was born in 1986 and Asperger's Syndrome didn't appear in the DSM-IV until 1994 brings up an interesting question regarding a strength- vs a deficit-based approach. (I also can't resist pointing out the importance of multilingualism in this context—though Hans Asperger had written about his research in the 1940s, his work wasn't translated into English until about 40 years later.) Had I known about Ben's Asperger's Syndrome earlier, would I still have chosen to give him a bilingual gifted education or simply have focused on his problems?

Though each parent must answer this question for him- or herself, in Ben's case, I see not knowing from the beginning as an unintended advantage. When his first few anomalies began to appear, I was much more likely to place a gifted rather than pathological interpretation on them—the enriched environment I tried to create emphasized strengths and expansiveness rather than narrow reductionism. This approach would enable me to see the positive side of many Asperger's characteristics once I learned more about the disorder.

Using *Bringing Up Baby Bilingual* as my blueprint, I proceeded on the next phase of the plan—expanding Ben's bilingual universe to include as many native speakers as possible, which also turned out to be a learning experience for me as well. Though I had spent years of my life studying and teaching French, my vocabulary leaned towards the literary. Thanks to the French Duden (a pictorial dictionary covering almost every conceivable aspect of human endeavor) and new French friends like Marie and Isabelle, I learned practical vocabulary like the word for "diaper" (*couche*).

Our new French friends became my teachers as well. For the first time, I began to understand the whole process of enculturation that a French person goes through from infancy. Huge gaps in my knowledge, despite residence and travel in France, began to be filled in. I learned what Marcel Proust's famous *tilleul* that inspired 13 volumes of reflections tasted like. And Ben had the advantage of experiencing both cultures from the inside from the beginning, as a normal part of his development.

I have often been asked how I managed to locate 40 French-speaking families in a town of around 20,000 people. Ben and I would meet a number of French nationals simply by walking down the street speaking French. It wasn't until years later I realized there was a certain irony to my situation. As a shy child, I never wanted to stand out or have people pay attention to me.

I preferred to observe, seemingly invisible, to blend into my surroundings chameleon-like, an ability which is useful in absorbing other languages and cultures but can prove damaging to the development of one's own identity. For some reason it never occurred to me that, by choosing to raise a French-speaking child in a small English-speaking town, I would immediately attract attention to me and my child. Getting used to this would later help me to deal with the attention attracted by the Asperger's. Years later one of the founders of LA Families with Children with Asperger's would say:

"You might as well get used to the fact that your child will always stand out."

So even from Ben's early days, I was unconsciously getting used to being on stage rather than watching from behind the scenes. The stage metaphor is particularly appropriate for someone living in Ashland, home of the Oregon Shakespeare Festival. What began as a decision to raise Ben bilingually would eventually, over the years, lead to creating a large network of people working on the possibility of a French immersion school, an Alliance Française, and a French sister-city relationship including theater exchanges.

I was finally using French in far more creative and enjoyable ways than I had when teaching elementary French grammar. This was one of the first examples of Ben acting as a catalyst in my life, bringing me into contact with larger numbers of French people, and bringing me experiences such as attending a multilingual international theater conference in Geneva. I, too, was immersed in French cultural activities and, despite the exhaustion of child-rearing, I felt much happier and more fully engaged than I had in years.

Ben's bilingualism was developing at a rapid rate. The Asperger's Syndrome anomalies developed gradually, sometimes giving Ben a certain advantage. Whereas some of my native-speaking friends' children were becoming passive bilinguals, understanding everything said to them in French but answering in English, Ben was a truly active bilingual, always speaking in French to French speakers. Here the intense focus of Asperger's Syndrome helped give Ben the ability to absorb vocabulary at an amazing rate with perfect native intonation.

A teacher from Besançon, France, who worked with him the summer before we went to France, made the following observation:

"I have to change the way I say 'Bonjour' every morning because he imitates my intonation exactly."

Over the years, I would learn how Ben could imitate with uncanny accuracy not only spoken words but any musical nuance, vocal or instrumental. He's told me, for example, that I laugh in the key of G. The reverse side of what involves both absolute pitch and Asperger's hyperacuity was Ben's extreme sensitivity to barking dogs and seat-belt signals on airplanes, which he's described as being in the keys of E flat or B flat. At this point, however, we simply assumed he had highly sensitive hearing.

On a trip to France, when Ben was age two and a half, another of his unusual characteristics emerged: a totally photographic memory. Ben had slept soundly on his first transatlantic flight, which we would regret on our arrival to Paris. He was wide awake, excitedly verbal when we got to the hotel. Ready to collapse from fatigue but concerned for the sleep of the other hotel guests, I took him into the bathroom where I had him talk in a whisper.

He proceeded to give me an astonishingly detailed account of one of our stroller walks in Ashland, not only including a full visual description but also quoting our entire conversation. When he described the public library, he related an entire "library story hour," including music, totally on pitch. What amazed me was the fact that during the actual experience, he hadn't appeared to be paying the slightest bit of attention yet had absorbed and retained everything.

This experience would be my first inkling of Ben's prodigious memory as well as his highly unusual way of learning any subject that interested him. Much later I would see a parallel between Ben's learning style and the total immersion method through which he had learned French—that he would completely immerse himself in any given subject, searching out experts until he had absorbed every conceivable bit of information.

At least two other unusual characteristics manifested themselves during the trip, which could later be seen as relating to the *idées fixes* of

Asperger's Syndrome. Early in our trip, we visited the home and laboratory of Louis Pasteur. Ben took everything in without too much comment. Later, when we went to Monet's home and gardens at Giverny he said:

"Ça, c'est la maison de Louis Pasteur." ("This is Louis Pasteur's home.")

"Non, c'est la maison de Claude Monet," I told him.

But Ben refused to change his mind, insisting on Louis Pasteur despite all evidence to the contrary.

A second example of inflexibility occurred when we began to sing the "Marseillaise" on a car ride with French friends. Because some of the pitches were slightly off, Ben insisted on singing solo, reflecting musical acuity coupled with social blindness, gift and challenge.

Having successfully negotiated Ben's first trip to France (with the additional help of my mother who came along for the first part), I was now re-energized to continue with the next step of his bilingual education, the development of a French immersion program for him to enter when he reached school age. To help publicize our project, Marie and I invited the assistant French cultural attaché to Ashland, organizing an entire week of French cultural activities in his honor.

He turned out to be a delightful young man, thoroughly appreciative of our efforts. He himself was a total bilingual, having spent part of his childhood in the US. He encouraged us to continue Ben's bilingual education, describing him as intelligent and friendly, already a native speaker of both languages.

In organizing the week, I needed to mobilize resources from diverse segments of the community, including city officials, the Chamber of Commerce, the Oregon Shakespeare Festival, the Ashland Public Library, and community volunteers. We put on a French children's film festival, an evening of French cultural activities (including a musical performance by our *petit groupe*). We organized a French drama and music evening in the park with actors from the Oregon Shakespeare Festival performing the scene from *Henry V* where Henry woos the French queen, replete with double entendres.

Everything in Ben's bilingual development appeared to be proceeding according to plan. But little did I realize that what seemed to be the "golden years" already contained seeds of darkness and difficult times that would slowly begin to dominate what had been a very positive picture.

Chapter Three

The fall after the assistant French cultural attaché's visit, Greg and I decided to place Ben in pre-school. Marie was forming an informal group in her home. In retrospect, I wonder if events would have unfolded differently had his first pre-school experience been with a familiar French speaker or if the French immersion program had reached fruition. As with alternative realities in science fiction, all I can do is speculate, having no way to try out the two different scenarios.

Reasoning that Ben had a solid enough grounding in French, we chose to put him in a regular American pre-school on the site of the college where both of us had taught. Since neither of us had attended pre-school and both had found adjustment to kindergarten difficult, we hoped to be giving Ben the advantage of earlier exposure to a class-room setting.

Within the first month, however, we started getting feedback that things weren't going "normally" from the teacher's point of view.

"Ben pays more attention to the mechanism of the water fountain than to circle time."

Both of us had grown up as fairly introverted intellectuals, never particularly relishing group time as children, and so observation didn't bother us. But we found an event a few months later truly alarming.

One day Ben managed to disappear from the pre-school, frightening in itself. But what disturbed us even more was that no one noticed he was gone. Luckily, a graduate student in psychology happened to see him wandering around and brought him back.

"I was looking for Papa," was Ben's perfectly logical explanation since Greg taught in a nearby building.

Later we would understand Ben's internal logic, with the intense focus of Asperger's Syndrome concentrating primarily on his father's whereabouts rather than issues of safety.

But at this point, we attributed Ben's escape partly to a lack of vigilance on the part of the staff. They, on the other hand, insisted it was impossible to keep track of him. We also had a bilingual basis for comparison with the weekly French group for children led by a teacher at the same site. Ben was one of the most active participants, never trying to escape. Since the pre-school setting was the same, we assumed the French language might well be a variable, a linguistic milieu in which he felt more comfortable.

We had a chance to test out this hypothesis when Greg received a Fulbright award to teach in France for 1991–2. Late summer, we set off for Besançon in eastern France, where Ben would spend a year in a French *école maternelle*. I was curious to see which factors of Ben's unusual profile would remain constant from the US and which would change once he was totally immersed in a French-speaking environment.

I had no apprehensions whatsoever about his ability to handle the French language. A lady on the bus, a few months into our stay, told me Ben had the gift for always finding *le mot juste*, the right word at a level far beyond what a five-year-old normally could handle. But after a month, I was called in for a conference with the teacher. I approached the conference both with dread, after Ben's US pre-school experience, and curiosity as to how cultural expectations might differ.

"His French is at native-speaking level," she told me, "with just one peculiarity. He uses the *tu* [you] form when speaking of himself rather than the first person."

Later, I was to find out that pronoun confusion could be one manifestation of Asperger's Syndrome.

The teacher continued. Though Ben had tried to leave class once, unlike in the American pre-school, his attempt was immediately noticed and stopped. She recommended a shorter day for him (4½ hours rather than 8!) and that he begin to play with children from the class outside of school (which also brought me into contact with their *mamans*). The rest of the year went fairly smoothly though Ben now tells me, with his photographic memory, of a year of terror, sometimes involving disciplinary measures such as slapping.

One bright spot was the *cantine* at school, the restaurant where he would eat multi-course French meals, ending with a cheese course. The friendly staff was determined to educate this young American in as many names of French cheeses as possible. This turned out to be a mixed blessing when we were invited out to people's houses for dinner. When we reached the cheese course, Ben would eye the selection, then mention the one cheese missing from the platter.

"Vous n'avez pas de Bleu d'Auvergne?" (You don't have any Bleu d'Auvergne?)

We had to apologize to our bewildered hosts, explaining about Ben's cheese lessons, but one can also interpret Ben's comment both as a tribute to his excellent memory and the challenge of social misunderstanding. Though I didn't completely realize it at the time, in addition to interpreting French language and culture for Ben, I was also interpreting social mores. Later, in the US, people would assume Ben didn't fully understand English when he appeared not to heed an instruction. What he experienced difficulty with, of course, was social rather than linguistic understanding.

Our year in France would prove to be my last year of psychological peace for at least a decade. On the surface, Ben appeared to be adjusting to school, spending time with his class on a nature weekend in the mountains near Switzerland. The French educational system seemed to be working better for him than the American. He was now becoming thoroughly immersed culturally as well as linguistically and passed for French despite slight anomalies in his behavior which people could ascribe to his youth and, when they found out his nationality, to differences in child-rearing practices.

I too was thriving, with time on my own to pursue my French theater research and the search for a sister city to Ashland. I had a chance to make a personal visit to a promising sister-city possibility, a small charming town in the south of France with a theater festival. I had also located my friend Michelle from Bordeaux during my Junior Year Abroad, now a psychologist in Marseille. Greg, Ben, and I traveled widely through France, deepening our knowledge of regional differences, making numerous friends.

Though prospects for a French immersion program had seemed bright when I left Ashland, during my absence, primarily due to an unfriendly administrator, the program had essentially been killed off. Despite broad community support, she had utilized one of the most effective ways of silencing innovative ideas—relegating them to a study committee with no decision-making authority. Formerly a political science major at Berkeley, I had now experienced an example of power politics in my own life.

I was amused, some years later, when Ben wrote the governor of Oregon about the variety of resources for Asperger's Syndrome in California. He received an answer saying Oregon was setting up an advisory committee.

"What does an advisory committee do?" he asked me.

"They can make recommendations," I answered.

"So they don't really have any power, right?" Ben concluded.

I have often marveled at an Asperger's person's ability to cut through layers of pretense to the underlying truth of the matter. We returned to Ashland with no French immersion program in place.

During our year in France, we had attempted to keep up Ben's English by reversing the process we'd used in Ashland of having French-speaking babysitters as much as possible. In Besançon we located American students in Junior Year Abroad programs who interacted with Ben in English. The fact that Ben had made it successfully through a year of French school helped raise my hopes that his American education could now go smoothly despite the lack of a

French immersion school to return to. I looked forward to continuing to have more time and energy to pursue my own life's directions as I had begun to do in France.

After my Bordeaux experience, I was prepared to experience some culture shock on returning to the US. But I assumed that, as an older married person, with a home base to return to, re-entry would come more easily. So though I left France regretfully, I felt physically, emotionally, spiritually recharged to return to Ashland, eager to continue working on the French sister city and other projects.

Instead, I was entering a dark tunnel through which I would travel for the next several years, a struggle between my vision of my child's potential and the limited resources of a small school district. The struggle would drive me to the absolute limits of my own inner resources. Though the French immersion program had fallen through, I had managed to locate a kindergarten teacher who had been raised bilingually and who I naïvely assumed would be more sympathetic to a bilingual/bicultural child. But within a few months, the questions began, carrying on from where they had left off before our year in France. Some of the comments didn't seem that problematic from our perspectives.

"Why does he keep answering us in French?"

"He's just returned from a year in France," I said, the answer seeming obvious.

"Why won't he participate in circle time?" came up again.

But this time, things went one step further as school personnel began to offer unsolicited possible diagnoses. Since Asperger's Syndrome wouldn't appear in the DSM-IV for another two years, they tried to fit Ben's differences into existing diagnoses that overlooked his gifts.

"Maybe he has epilepsy and is having minor seizures and that's why he doesn't listen. Possibly Severely Emotionally Disturbed?"

We couldn't reconcile what we were hearing with the intelligent, musical, bilingual boy we continued to observe. We struggled all year with the contradiction between our perception of Ben's strengths and the school's picture of dysfunction. At the suggestion of a child therapist friend to have Ben assessed privately, we took him to a local psychologist.

"He's smart, ready for first grade but a little behind socially," she said, "possibly because of bilingualism. Of course, what you want is for Ben to become a typical American boy."

"Not exactly," I thought, but didn't have the courage to say out loud at this point, not being a mental health professional. Though her observations relieved my mind, I still firmly believed in a multilingual, multicultural education. I'm grateful I had the strength of my beliefs not to change my bilingual approach. I have since heard of other cases where an Asperger's Syndrome child was switched to monolingualism with an increase rather than decrease of symptoms.

As the year went on, I began to relive the pain of my own primary and secondary education, a period I had never wanted to revisit. Part of the reason I had chosen to raise Ben with an innovative approach had been to try to avoid the alienation and struggle I had experienced until Berkeley. I sought to create a more nurturing environment in which he might flourish. Instead, Ben appeared to be deviating from the norm even more radically than I. I, albeit "suffering in silence," had at least been able to blend in, "pass," on the surface. Ben's differences, however, were manifesting themselves far more visibly, with no chance of hiding.

Some parents, at this point, would have chosen to give up the struggle and agree to whatever the school personnel came up with, no matter how inappropriate. Either I could ignore my own perceptions and beliefs and accept uncritically the school's deficit-oriented focus or I could stand up for an alternative view of my child, one focusing on strengths as well as challenges. I chose the latter course, persevering in coming up with resources that would address Ben's anomalies from the perspective of his positive potential. This would mean a considerable investment of time and energy on my part.

I started coming into Ben's class on a regular basis to do French language and music, hoping to build a bridge between Ben's worlds (with the added benefit of giving the other children some exposure to a second language). Despite the teacher's habit of constantly interrupting and asking me to translate, contrary to the immersion model, I managed to make it through the year.

Following the French *école maternelle* model of having Ben socialize with other children outside the classroom, every week I invited one of the families to share a French dinner with us. Though all accepted our invitation, only one person ever reciprocated by agreeing to have Ben come over while I was on jury duty. Even at this early stage, we began to feel the social stigma and ostracism of having a child who was different.

One mother was even tactless enough to state this overtly when I was trying to arrange a play date for Ben with her son. She asked her child while I was on the phone and he refused.

"Isn't it amazing," she told me, "how even in kindergarten kids decide who they like and who they don't?"

Her thoughtless words reopened my years of social rejection but I persevered, organizing a birthday party, including other children in activities. I supplemented Ben's education with a gifted education tutor who wrote weekly reports, which I'd bring into the dreaded, ever more frequent meetings at his school.

I was beginning to discover, to my chagrin, that once the school district adopted a particular pathological mindset about a child, it was very hard to change that mindset despite any additional information to the contrary that parents brought in. Ben was blissfully unaware of the growing pressure on us and views his kindergarten year as one of his happiest (though he didn't communicate this at the time).

Yet by fighting for my child's rights, I was beginning a process of change in myself as well. I had been given a second chance, after the unquestioning attitude of my own schooling, to propose a more creative approach. But to assert a different vision of my child to the school, I had to overcome my own shyness and fear of being on center stage.

I had done this in my French activities, including acting in French as a graduate student. But to take on what could become an adversarial position, I needed to face my fear of overtly disagreeing with people. I was well aware I was neither a mental health professional nor an elementary school teacher. I was now entering an arena where, as with bilingualism, I had to rely in large part on my own faith that the seeds of positive potential in my child could be nurtured and would one day flourish.

In the summer of 1993 we returned to France to work on theater exchanges. Again, we experienced the odd sensation, after the pressures and worries of Ben's kindergarten year, of having our child considered "normal." French people continued to enjoy Ben's perfect grasp of the language, his familiarity with their culture. His difficulties with the American school system began to seem like a momentary aberration attributable to cross-cultural differences.

For the fall, in an attempt to isolate potential environmental variables, we decided to transfer Ben to his neighborhood school, hoping that this way, he'd have a better chance to get to know kids who lived nearby. I naïvely assumed he'd really have a chance for a fresh start in a new school, not fully appreciating that in a small school district, there are no secrets.

I would later find out that observations were being recorded on Ben from the beginning (including, at times, gratuitous unprofessional comments about us as well). Ben's "dossier" reflected only the school district's view. Virtually none of our information on Ben's ability, such as reports from the gifted tutor, made it in. Unbeknown to us, his kindergarten teacher paid a visit during the summer to his new teacher to fill her in on what she saw as Ben's anomalies.

Unaware of all this, I'd chosen a first-grade teacher who seemed very enthusiastic about my coming into the classroom to do French. In my eagerness to have things run more smoothly than they had the previous year, I tended to gloss over or totally overlook early indications of potential problems.

What seemed like a creative classroom atmosphere (multiple activity centers) might also help create sensory chaos in a susceptible person. I did notice a marked contrast between the teacher's exuberant personality and that of the reserved classroom aide.

This time, however, I didn't even have a month's reprieve. Within a week of the beginning of school, the familiar complaints began as a year unfolded, even more problematic than the previous one.

Chapter Four

Despite Ben's anomalies, however, Ben's teacher had to admit he was also beginning to show some remarkable abilities. He exhibited a highly unusual learning style. During reading lessons, he appeared to be paying little or no attention to the instruction.

"He's one of the strongest readers and spellers in the class," the teacher told us. "But he hardly ever looks at the board. We can't figure out how he's learning."

Part of the answer probably lay in Ben's extraordinary auditory ability and photographic memory. But, as we were to discover, there's always been an element in Ben's learning style that defies comprehension. Once he becomes interested in a subject, he very quickly amasses an encyclopedic knowledge of it. After being told the names of a few trees, for example, within a couple of months he had learned huge numbers of species, both in French and English.

I'd ordered French reading materials from France, which arrived a few months after Ben had learned to read in English. Soon after we began working with them, Ben asked me:

"Is the letter 'h' pronounced in written French?"

When I told him no, he picked up a French book and proceeded to read a page correctly in French.

But despite evidence that Ben had gifts as well as challenges, school officials continued to focus solely on the pathological (an approach which, I would discover, was also funding driven). Unfortunately, though funding for special education is written into the law, support for gifted education is either discretionary or non-existent. The pressures for psychological testing grew.

Following a therapist friend's advice, we had Ben assessed privately. In a pattern that would repeat itself numerous times, Ben refused to follow test instructions. Instead, he studied the system of flashing red lights used to call the next client. This led the psychologist, still in pre-Asperger's Syndrome days, to speak of Ben's "psychotic tendencies," frightening terminology but seeming still more off-base than epilepsy, even to someone without a degree in psychology. I did, however, decide, to have Ben begin seeing a therapist.

In an unorthodox way, I chose one, Sue, who worked out of her home. When she mentioned she did Jungian sand tray work, I immediately had to see the playroom.

"Usually I speak with the parents first but we can do it in the other order as well."

I liked her flexibility, which would prove to be invaluable in the turbulent years that would follow. As I entered the playroom, myriad microcosms opened up before me. I saw miniature figurines from different historical periods and cultures—knights and ladies, trees in different seasons, gemstones, waterfalls, animals, real and mythological. There was so much diversity I couldn't take it all in on one visit—pleasant sensory overload.

I had experienced a similar sensation as when we arrived in Ashland and I'd looked at the endless green waves of forest through the cabin window. I knew Sue's workspace also held infinite potential, that within it there would be room and diversity enough to explore the mystery of Ben. Though I didn't realize it initially, I was also choosing my own therapist. Searching out resources for Ben, time after time, would also lead me to resources for my own growth.

Sue was the one bright spot in a year that grew more and more polarized. The outside social pressures were now beginning to affect our marriage. As someone told me recently:

"A disorder in a family member can affect the family in one of two ways. It can either bring the family members closer together or drive them further apart."

Different people respond differently to stress. Ben's school difficulties also elicited painful memories in Greg of his own childhood conflicts. With the day-to-day task of raising a challenging child, and the situation with the school, we had little time and space for our own lives and relating as a couple.

Often, the only opportunity we had for discussions came during long car trips with Ben present. Ben remembers vividly our talks on how to deal with him, often lasting for hours on long car trips between Oregon and California. I now regret we talked about Ben in the third person, as if he weren't there. We also had no idea he would remember the exact time, place, and subject of every discussion, the curse of a photographic memory.

Years later, Ben would ask questions like:

"Why on March 17, 1993 at rest area 265 did you and my father disagree on how to raise me?"

Greg and I had little time alone to speak since the school's solution, as soon as any problems arose with Ben, was to have me come pick him up (thus reinforcing the idea that all he had to do was act up to get sprung from an uncomfortable environment). In the most extreme case, I would drop him off at 8.30 a.m. only to be called by 9.30 a.m. to pick him up. I never knew when the dreaded phone call would come, interrupting my writing.

I found myself on what, at first, appeared to be a lonely, painful road. I was entering an ordeal by fire, which would ultimately transform me into a much stronger person.

As Ben's difficult first-grade year drew to a close, an unexpected ally appeared associated with bilingualism. All year, I'd been bringing up bilingualism as an important variable and finally we were offered an assessment by a bilingual specialist, which we immediately agreed to.

The specialist didn't return my call before meeting Ben, wanting to draw her own conclusions. She later told me the district had instructed her to "come up with results that back us up," advice she had fortunately ignored, preferring to conduct as unbiased an assessment as possible.

After Robyn worked with Ben, she suggested we meet in person to discuss the results. A woman with clear, intelligent eyes walked towards me and to my surprise, gave me a hug. Her first words astonished me even more.

"I want to discuss the possibility with you that your child is gifted."

At first, I could hardly speak, as great waves of emotion surged through me. For so long now, I had persisted in believing in Ben's positive potential despite ever growing pressure to focus only on problems. More and more, I had only my own faith in Ben to rely on. Robyn's words, for the first time, provided a validation of my intuitions from an outside professional. I felt a mixture of relief, joy, and accumulated sadness at having been so alone for such a long time. When I could finally speak, I thanked her.

"No one's ever told me that before. You can't imagine what this means to me."

"Of all the bilingual children I've ever assessed, Ben scored the highest, his answers went far beyond what the test asked for."

She described how Ben, when shown a picture of a submarine, started speculating on the degree of condensation on the portholes.

"I want you to spend the summer doing as much research as possible on giftedness and bilingualism," she told me. "I think this is the direction we'll need to move in this fall."

I sensed a new road was opening up, hitherto outside my field of perception, a road much more congruent with my observations of and feelings about my child. In retrospect I realize that the choice to raise Ben bilingually led me, through Robyn, to begin to learn about giftedness. I can only wonder otherwise when and if we would have ever discovered gifted education.

Part of the new territory we were beginning to find ourselves in was the border between gifted and special education, where often little communication or "cultural exchange" takes place. Though I have met very idealistic people over the years in both fields, I have also met a number who have difficulty with the concept that someone can be gifted and have challenges at the same time. Ironically, some of the educational and psychological professionals who are supposed to be dealing with the inflexibility of Asperger's Syndrome are themselves displaying a similar inflexibility in their inability to consider "both/and" rather than "either/or."

Robyn told me of numerous cases where bilingual children had been consigned to special education, their only "disability" being not speaking English. A number of these children, placed in severely developmentally disabled classes, ended up being identified as gifted bilinguals. Later, when I spoke to a special education teacher about the lack of resources for gifted and bilingual children with unusual learning styles, she blurted out:

"I know, Special Ed. is full of these kids."

As Ben entered second grade, my research into bilingualism and giftedness began to give me a fuller picture of who Ben was, a counterbalance to continuing pressure from the district (which also consistently refused to state which resources they had in mind for him). As a bilingual child, Ben became eligible for tutors, college students who spent a term working with bilinguals as part of their education. Displeased with the fact Robyn's assessment, rather than backing up the district, had presented an alternative picture, the same administrator who had wiped out French immersion tried unsuccessfully to get Ben decertified as a bilingual, hoping to force us to accept whatever the district offered.

"You need to contact Dr. June Maker in Arizona," Robyn told us. "She's one of the country's leading specialists on bilingual giftedness."

I called Dr. Maker and she told me her team would be happy to assess Ben in French. When I finally met Dr. Maker in person, I asked her how she had become interested in the area of bilingual giftedness.

"I started out by studying children who had been labeled 'learning disabled' yet showed definite signs of giftedness."

She described how she had started with a "both/and" rather than an "either/or" model, that new assessment instruments needed to be developed for children with both exceptionalities.

"When I moved to Arizona," she told me, "I extended the learning disabled/gifted model to bilingual children whose giftedness had often been overlooked by the use of linguistically and culturally biased assessments."

She and her team developed instruments that could be utilized with children from any linguistic background. I feel the "both/and" model of giftedness and challenges offers great promise for children with Asperger's Syndrome with their unique, often extraordinary areas of giftedness. Somehow a dialogue needs to develop between Gifted and Special Education (which, ironically, are often housed in the same academic department).

We returned to Ashland with data showing Ben's bilingual giftedness in a number of areas. Finally, I thought, we can present the district with independent professional corroboration of what I'd been saying for three years now. But when I brought in the University of Arizona data, I saw, to my horror, they wrote down "parental information" (translation: "emotionally biased, disregard").

Meanwhile, Ben lacked a workable program addressing both his abilities and challenges. One day, I received a highly unprofessional call from the administrator who had tried to get Ben decertified as a bilingual.

"Susan, I'm so mad at you," she screamed at me.

"Well, I'm not mad at you," I began in all honesty.

My response made her even angrier and she hung up on me.

Two other incidents occurred before the year's end, which I find shocking both for their cruelty and lack of respect for confidentiality and parents' feelings. The retired aide who helped the teacher shouted after me one day in the hallway, within earshot of other parents, teachers, and students:

"It's obvious Ben is Severely Emotionally Disturbed."

I couldn't believe that someone with professional therapeutic training could be so unprofessional as to shout out a presumed diagnosis in public.

Shortly afterwards, another school aide wrote an article in the school's newspaper, denouncing our independent course of action, identifying us in every way but by name. When I complained to the principal about both incidents, she agreed that neither was appropriate and promised to have a retraction printed, which never happened. Even if one had appeared, the damage was already done, as when a lawyer who "accidentally" mentions a factor in court he or she knows will advance the case: though the lawyer is ruled out of order and the jury are urged to disregard the information, obviously they heard what was said and can't erase it from their memories during their deliberations.

By the end of summer, we had entered mediation with the district. I was still naïve enough to believe we would get a fair hearing and be able to come up with a strength-based program for Ben. I had underestimated the weight (literal and figurative by this point) of his dossier, containing almost daily behavioral observations gathered without parental permission, data interpreted to prove pathology without showing the full spectrum of the child's personality. No one informed us in advance of the mediation of our right to read his dossier (though all other parties had done so).

When I later found out about my rights and had a chance to read Ben's records, one of the most hurtful discoveries was a letter from a "gifted education specialist" we had brought into mediation. Based on her reading of the dossier without our knowledge, she recommended having Ben assessed by a psychologist friend of hers whom she would advise to come up with an emotionally disturbed diagnosis. She also included a gratuitous personal attack against me for not accepting the district's conclusions. We were playing cards with a deck stacked against us. An agreement was negotiated, theoretically dealing with both Ben's gifts and challenges.

Implementation, however, was another question. Third grade began with a person (not agreed to in the mediation) following Ben around. Within four days, the agreement had broken down (after numerous escape attempts on Ben's part). The district suspended Ben and sent him home. Though legally a suspension was only supposed to last for four days, they refused to take Ben back and said they would eventually send a home teacher five hours a week.

With no advance notice and without our conscious intention, we had become involuntary home-schoolers. But in Mandarin Chinese, the character for crisis is also the character for opportunity. Looked at creatively, every seeming obstacle can afford an opportunity for new growth. Reaching a brick wall, you can either continue banging your head fruitlessly against it or explore a different direction. What turned into a long period of home-schooling taught us a great deal about Ben's learning style, about what worked, and what didn't. Years later, I would hear Dr. Tony Attwood say that home-schooling often provided one of the best models for children with Asperger's Syndrome.

What didn't work was immediately apparent. Trying to have Ben do someone else's curriculum (reading, math, etc.) resulted in a great deal of resistance and little finished work. (This may have related to his global rather than sequential learning style as well as his personality.) Yet once Ben generated the topic and modality, he could proceed at amazing speed.

The previous summer in France, I'd bought Ben a French children's book on bicycle repair. As if by Jungian synchronicity, the tutor Robyn had found happened to work at a bike shop and had spent part of his childhood in French-speaking Belgium. So part of Ben's initial home-schooling included learning how to ride a bicycle in French.

Over the next four years, Ben would cover a wide variety of subjects including horticulture and simulated rock-climbing (we would always try to utilize the particular interests and strengths of the individual tutor as well). With additional French-speaking tutors I located, Ben learned French cooking, skiing, tennis, and some chess, totally in French. We had inadvertently stumbled on the experiential education approach, which worked much better for Ben at this stage than a conventional classroom.

The district provided a teacher who, we soon discovered, had been put in an unenviable position. They had instructed her to keep behavioral notes on Ben, and to try to recreate anomalous situations to see if he would run away etc. Even though Ben was no longer physically attending school, the district seemed unable to give up its reductionistic mindset, which focused only on problems rather than providing a more balanced approach. We were able to change teachers to a French teacher on leave who formulated a creative program utilizing Ben's strengths in French and his interests.

Before Ben's suspension, I had arranged to bring a teaching assistant from France to work at his school, who spent a number of hours a week with Ben at home. She supplemented other facets of his education by teaching him lovely French cursive (as exemplified in the Babar books). Though Ben could reproduce French cursive, he continued printing in English, explaining that cursive was just for French. This explanation probably came from a mixture of his unique learning style, as well as an Asperger's tendency towards compartmentalization, and a rather stubborn personality.

We somehow managed to make it through what would have been Ben's third-grade year. On the plus side, I no longer had to deal with dropping him off at 8.30 only to be called to pick him up an hour later. We *did* have a chance to explore some creative approaches with resources available. But "resources available" still meant only a few hours off a day for me and I was left with most of the work, on a scale I'd never imagined.

Whereas most parents can count on several hours a day of free time once their child enters school, my life had taken exactly the opposite course. I now found myself assuming the roles of part-time teacher, therapist, respite person, gifted education program planner, social/recreational aide, bilingual resource person to name just a few. All summer, I persisted in looking for alternatives, no easy task in a small town of 20,000 people.

The Waldorf School agreed to give Ben a try in fourth grade. He began with one hour a week, one-on-one with the teacher. As would prove to be the case many times, Ben enjoyed working individually with a resource person. He would ply the person with innumerable questions, which, we learned, was one of his most effective ways of amassing knowledge.

But when the transition to the classroom came in the spring, the situation quickly changed. Though Ben liked the farm setting and the kids, he was highly reluctant to learn according to a set curriculum, which in Waldorf education follows a very specific pattern.

"But I don't want to study about cuttlefish," he protested one day, the subject not falling into his current area of interest, which happened to be botany.

Though Ben enjoyed his four months at Waldorf, his unwilling-ness to follow the curriculum plus a large increase in class size led to the need to search out yet another alternative for the following year. We found out about a home-schooling/independent study program where we could receive funding to hire a teacher. My French friend Isabelle, a former actress, developed a program where she would work one-on-one with Ben as well as doing a weekly drama workshop in French with three other bilingual home-schooled children to try to expand his social network.

In many ways, the crisis of Ben leaving public school had brought the opportunity of exploring alternative forms of education. But our rupture with the school district had also brought with it the loss of a very deep friendship.

We had been delighted to meet Catherine when Ben was in second grade, as his musical ability and interest became more and more apparent. Catherine was not only a music teacher but also a native speaker of French. She readily accepted the opportunity to teach Ben music in French. Ben greatly enjoyed his lessons with Catherine, whose good humor and kindness impressed me as well. Though also employed by the district as a music teacher, Catherine seemed sympa-thetic to my efforts to develop an alternative program for Ben, describ-ing her own experience partly home-schooling her own child.

I now had found a creative resource person with whom to share ideas in French. Catherine was a total bilingual and could provide me with a great deal of helpful information on raising Ben bilingually as well.

My exchanges with France reawakened an interest in the culture for Catherine. She joined the French singing group, which met periodically at my house, and we would converse frequently on the progress of the exchanges. I viewed her not only as a resource person who shared many of Ben's interests, but also as a trusted friend with whom I could share many of mine.

In the aftermath of mediation, she had offered to serve on a parent/school team trying to come up with some kind of a program for Ben. Theoretically, she thought she could play the role of bridging the district's perspective and ours, as well as being able to speak from her own knowledge of Ben's abilities in French and music. In retrospect, I see two telling comments, which foreshadowed the course of events.

She told me once, laughing: "In any fight between parents and a school district, the district always wins."

I found her comment a little cynical, thinking: "Not in Ben's case."

Then, at one of our meetings, the presiding administrator looked directly at Catherine.

"What a wonderful channel you are to the family," she told her.

Something about the intensity of her tone made me uncomfortable. I also found it unusual she referred to us impersonally as "the family" almost as if we weren't physically present at the meeting.

When we arrived for Ben's next lesson, I could immediately sense a change in Catherine's conversational tone. Without our usual friendly, relaxed exchange, she immediately thrust a large stack of xeroxes in my face.

"Here, read this. Once you're done, we'll schedule a meeting."

Puzzled by Catherine's formal terminology of "scheduling a meeting," I took the papers and read the words "Asperger's Syndrome" for the first time. As I was later to learn, the district had indeed used Catherine as a "wonderful channel of communication with the family" in a way that involved deception and mistrust, and guaranteed the end of a friendship.

The district's methods present a perfect model about how not to communicate with parents about a possible disorder. I can fully understand how a person with Asperger's Syndrome feels when information is conveyed in an overly emotional way—the tendency is to focus on the emotional affect rather than the information. Before I could even give the articles a fair hearing, I had to digest the district's duplicity and how my friend had been used. The methods the district used to accelerate a process actually had the opposite effect of postponing my further research into Asperger's Syndrome.

I was supposed to believe that Catherine, a music teacher, not a psychologist, just happened to be browsing through the library and had found information on Asperger's Syndrome, which had just appeared for the first time in the DSM-IV—not, I would guess, customary reading for someone in music. Even before I had a chance to read the information and give my opinion, it had already been passed on to the home teacher the district initially sent. Her reaction was highly revealing:

"Ben's former classroom teacher was a good person and the district got to her. Catherine was a good person and they got to her. I wonder who they'll get to next?"

The next time I saw Catherine, I told her I'd skimmed the information and found it interesting but that it didn't seem to correspond to many parts of Ben, including his musical giftedness and bilingualism.

"He's just a good mimic, that's all," were Catherine's words.

I found myself speechless and deeply hurt at this total reversal of position in a trusted friend who had consistently supported an alternative view of Ben, praising his amazing abilities in music and French.

"I'm in complete agreement with the district, now," she said.

"But even if we have different perspectives, we can still separate your relationship with Ben as a music teacher and continue his lessons."

"I can't separate the two and can't teach him any more."

She refused to see Ben again, even to say good-bye, to achieve closure. I felt the multiple loss of an excellent resource person and a close friend though I now recognize her difficulty of having to chose between her position as a school district employee and friendship. Just as Ben's music was beginning to take off and we had finally found a compatible teacher, that door was slammed in our faces.

Yet the end of this road actually turned out to be the beginning of a new one. Had Catherine not dropped Ben as a pupil, we never would have embarked on a search for a new teacher which would ultimately lead us to Dave, who continues to play a significant role in our lives to this day.

Chapter Five

Early on with Ben, I learned to be aware of when a window opened in his mind through which new knowledge and experience could enter. We had taken Ben to hear folksinger Tom Paxton, and he expressed interest in learning how to play the guitar. As we researched music teachers and tried sample lessons, we found that few teachers could cope with Ben's unusual learning style. Then I learned about Dave Marston. I'd remembered Dave as head of the Green Show at the Oregon Shakespeare Festival but had always thought of him as a vocalist specializing in Renaissance music rather than a guitar teacher.

With some trepidation after our previous experiences, I called Dave and described Ben. To my surprise, Dave gave an enthusiastic response.

"He sounds fascinating. I'm really looking forward to meeting him."

Dave told me he had a three-month waiting list but to keep calling back. Finally there was an opening and Ben showed up for his first lesson. Though he avidly watched and listened to Dave, he refused to pick up his guitar.

"Here we go again," I thought.

But Dave's reaction took me by surprise.

"That's OK," he said. "Keep on bringing the guitar and eventually he'll start playing."

Dave's faith in the process inspired me to continue. For about three months, Ben simply observed. Then when he finally picked up the guitar, he quickly amassed a thorough knowledge of nearly all the chords and strums.

"Show me a D diminished seventh," he would ask Dave.

Ben liked Dave so much that we started taking him to Dave's monthly Beatles singalongs. Ben learned one Beatles song then proceeded to learn all 208, after requesting the most obscure ones possible at the singalongs.

Dave pointed out that Ben wasn't just satisfied with a basic knowledge of each song. Instead, he insisted on duplicating each vocal and instrumental nuance exactly as the Beatles performed them, even trying to make his child's voice sound lower. We would later see this ability transferred to the work of Bob Dylan, Woody Guthrie, Bill Staines etc. Dave was open to letting Ben set the agenda for his lessons, delighted to have a student who shared his love for the Beatles.

I observed Dave's teaching style with great awe and admiration, marveling at his clarity and patience. In my musical experience, I had seen many musicians who were good performers but poor teachers and vice versa. Dave is the rare combination of excellent performer and excellent teacher.

Little did I realize at first what an important role Dave would play in my own life as well. Like Ben, I would find myself moving from observer to participant. One day Ben brought in a song Dave wasn't familiar with so Ben and I sang a duet. When we were finished, Dave said something that both amazed and pleased me.

"You have a very nice voice."

"Thank you," I managed to say, tears welling up.

No one had ever complimented me on my singing before. I'd assumed that my sister Lois was the one with the good voice, that though I loved singing, I was forever relegated to the instrumental ranks. To be complimented by a musician I greatly respected gave me the courage to verbalize a secret wish I'd harbored for years.

"I've always wanted to take voice lessons," I told him. "Would you have room for another student?"

"Of course."

So a month shy of my birthday in 1996, I began to study voice and, for the first time, music started to become something other than an ambivalent experience for me. We began with Renaissance songs, then Thomas Morley duets, French, Russian, Ladino folk songs. With Dave's gentle but persistent manner, I felt encouraged to explore new areas; I learned I didn't have to achieve instant perfection in breathing technique, placing a tone. I found my self-consciousness leaving me as I entered fully into the music. Gradually, music was becoming a joyous experience for me. I began to realize Dave was helping me open emotional channels as well as musical.

The following spring, Dave, Ben, and I performed at a birthday celebration for Greg's mother. One guest commented:

"Susan has finally found her voice."

Finding my musical voice would extend to other areas as well. As our situation in Ashland became more and more difficult, music helped sustain me psychologically, bringing some light and release into the gathering darkness. A birthday trip to Australia provided momentary respite from increasing stresses both within and without—marital stress in addition to a return to home-schooling in the aftermath of Waldorf.

The trip to Australia would be the last purely enjoyable vacation we ever spent as a family. We traveled as a cross-generational group, including my mother and my 17-year-old niece, Hannah. I turned 50 on Kangaroo Island where I sang a Renaissance song, "Since First I saw Your Face," carrying Dave's music across the ocean.

We took off for Ashland from New Zealand, leaving in the middle of a cyclone which pursued us across the ocean. The storm continued on the west coast, eventually closing down Ashland's water system for two weeks. And the figurative storm of our existence continued to intensify.

Isabelle worked very creatively with Ben in French, incorporating Waldorf elements and art therapy, to which he responded in their one-on-one sessions. But when the other French-speaking children came over, he refused to participate. Meanwhile, his botanical obsession continued to grow, leading him into potentially dangerous areas.

Though he had amassed an amazing body of knowledge in French and English on trees, he had developed a curious obsession which has defied professional understanding to this day. Unable to simply observe the change in seasons, he felt compelled to speed them along. As soon as the leaves began to turn, he would rip them off the trees. An excellent climber, he could reach perilous heights, oblivious to any potential danger.

Once that he had turned our garden into premature winter, he took the dangerous step, physically and legally, of venturing beyond our yard into the neighbors' trees. One day, I returned to find poor Isabelle trying to talk him down from a tall ash whose thin branches were bending precariously, even under his slight weight.

No amount of redirecting could stop him. I was now faced with the double burden of continuing to search out resources to nourish his gifts plus keeping him out of danger. When Sue tried to find out why he continued to rip leaves off trees, all he would say was:

"I want the seasons to go faster."

The compulsion waned during the winter, only to return in full intensity in the spring when he went after the blossoms. Though Ben had a total understanding of the botanical growth cycle, and had many conversations with the park horticulturist, he seemed unable to stop his destructive actions. Outdoor walks, formerly enjoyable for both of us, became impossible.

Trying to add in a new element, I searched for a social skills person, reasoning if Ben become more comfortable with groups, he would pay less attention to the leaves. In Tina, however, I found much more than a social skills person. Tina also had a Master's degree in theology and had home-schooled her own gifted son. She was open-minded, creative, enthusiastic about the idea of working with Ben. By the end of spring, she agreed to begin home-teaching him in the fall.

That summer, we returned to France, little imagining this would be our last trip to the country as a family. For the first time, the normal/abnormal dichotomy of our French/American lives began to break down. The nightmare of Ben's problems crossed over into France.

Our difficulties began with the journey over. Though we'd accumulated enough mileage for free tickets, the only route available involved a total of four flights including a transfer in Canada. Ever since Ben's first transatlantic flight in 1989, we'd noticed him covering his ears when traveling on planes, which we'd assumed was associated with air pressure changes. But as his hyperacuity/absolute pitch became more apparent and his verbal ability developed, he articulated that he was bothered by the bells on the planes (which, he informed us, rang either in B flat or E flat). Even before we'd left North America, he was highly anxious about the seatbelt signals.

I tried my best to calm him down (having to ignore my own fear of flying, which my love of travel counterbalances). I had to talk Ben down enough to get him on the last flight to Paris (by mentioning some of his favorite French food).

Somehow, we made it to France. Part of our time seemed normal and enjoyable. With a wonderful French friend and her great-nieces, we traveled to Lorient, Brittany, to attend the world's largest Celtic music festival. Despite his hyperacuity, Ben was able to tolerate an orchestra of 450 bagpipes.

But later in the trip, we encountered the French equivalent of "how not to speak with parents." This time, a French acquaintance with whom we were spending a few days didn't even bother to speak to me in private about Ben as Catherine had done. Instead, she chose to share her opinions at a meal in a café with about 15 of her friends present. Loudly, in earshot of all including Ben she said:

"Everyone's noticed how strangely Ben behaves, even more so than you'd expect with Americans who let their children do whatever they want. There's something wrong with him and he needs to be sent to a special school for children with problems."

I didn't know where or how to begin to respond—by saying how embarrassed I was by the public nature of her pronouncements, or by speaking to the content, the affect, the stereotyped assumptions about American child-rearing practices. Earlier in the visit, she'd told me I was being too cautious with Ben, that I should let him wander freely (towards leaves etc.). I experienced the unpleasant phenomenon I'd encountered in the US of being damned if you do, damned if you don't, often receiving contradictory advice from the same person. This attitude can also be summarized as:

"In the presence of unusual behavior, blame the parents."

I had already been blamed for Ben's behavior because of initially raising him as vegetarian and as bilingual, as failing to provide discipline, etc. It didn't seem to occur to anyone offering "helpful advice," that simply dealing with such a challenging child on a daily basis might be extremely difficult and exhausting. Few people seemed to realize that acknowledging my feelings and offering support might be more helpful than leveling superficial criticism. I also felt saddened that France, at least in this case, no longer represented a refuge.

We returned to the US more exhausted than renewed. In the fall of 1997, Ben's botanical obsession led him into personal danger. On October 14 he celebrated his 11th birthday with a wonderful Beatles singalong led by Dave. The next day, in pursuit of autumn leaves, he fell out of a tree, breaking his right wrist.

He ended up in a cast for several weeks, a sad fate for anyone but devastating for a musician. Ironically, my father and I, both musicians, had also broken our right wrists in accidents. Both of us had had to go through the long process of rehabilitation to regain enough flexibility to begin playing instruments again. In his determination to continue his lessons with Dave, Ben somehow managed to play guitar in a cast and talked the doctor into removing it a few weeks early.

Around this time, Isabelle proposed something that at first terrified me.

"Let's do a public concert together of French music in December."

She mentioned the little theater her ex-husband ran as a possible venue. Though I'd been studying with Dave for a year now, my initial reaction reflected my performance anxiety with the violin. But this time, while acknowledging my fear, I decided I was ready to move past it.

"I'll give it a try," I told Isabelle, "but I'd like Dave to coach us."

Therein began a wonderful collaboration. Though Dave doesn't know French, he helped us with harmonies, accompaniments, vocal technique; it represented a welcome change from the day-to-day struggles of the other parts of my life. We rehearsed stage movement as well, an aspect of performance I'd never been fully aware of before.

We performed to an enthusiastic audience and I felt an enormous sense of fulfillment at having surmounted one of my psychological barriers. I had finally had the courage to assume center stage for myself, to share my enjoyment of French music with others. Again, Ben had served as an indirect catalyst in my own development since I had met both Dave and Isabelle in my search for resource people for him.

Our concert was one of the only positive experiences in a period of ever-gathering darkness (as well as being a step along my own path into activities not directly involving my child). In the fall, I'd organized a meeting of all the people working with Ben—Sue, Dave, Isabelle, Robyn—and, in an optimistic spirit, we planned to coordinate our efforts.

By May, when we met again, this time adding in Tina, the picture was more mixed. Dave and Isabelle spoke of some of Ben's resistance when it came to doing music and drama with other kids (though he continued to enjoy working with them one-on-one).

During the summer, we took Ben to a psychiatrist in San Francisco who specialized in musically gifted children and was also bilingual in French and English. He noticed a curious tendency of Ben's:

"He's switching me at will between French and English," he said, an early indication of Ben's ability to instantly psych people out and play them like chess pieces. He mentioned Asperger's Syndrome as one possibility. We also had Ben evaluated by a neurologist who wanted him tested for Fragile X.

Tina was running into Ben's resistance towards any sort of home-schooling techniques. His leaf obsession was growing so intense, she could no longer take him out alone and drive safely. What little "off-time" I had had now vanished completely, as I started accompanying them. For three months, I had tried to make an appointment with a child psychiatrist (there were only two for a three-county area of over 100,000 people). Though Ben's Fragile X test turned out negative, the Denver center thought they could help him so I was making arrangements to visit in the late fall.

Meanwhile I was involved in putting on a conference that would bring Dr. June Maker, the Arizona bilingual gifted specialist, to Ashland. I barely managed to get help with Ben for a few hours to attend. I also had the painful task of doing Ben's 12th birthday party, attempting to entertain the guests while Ben headed up trees, madly ripping off leaves.

Unable to get even a call back from the local child psychiatrists, I contacted the child psychiatrist we had seen in San Francisco, describing Ben's symptoms.

"I can't tell if it's Asperger's or OCD [obsessive compulsive disorder]," he said, "but we can try an OCD medication."

Anafranil, as it turned out, made Ben's behavior even more extreme. Now he was trying to leave the house at 2 a.m. to rip off leaves. I had to install new locks and hide the keys, which Ben would frantically try to find. On November 11, when Ben and I were driving and he was talking incessantly, I sideswiped a car, the first moving violation in my entire driving history. Then, on November 22, the anniversary of the Kennedy assassination, I went through the most nightmarish weekend of my life.

Chapter Six

After the June Maker conference, my mother, Ben, and I planned to drive north to Grant's Pass to spend what I hoped would be a relaxing weekend by the river. Very quickly, we began to find ourselves immersed in a series of events that resembled the unfolding of a frightening film in which we were present as actors, not spectators. My only parallel experience was the birth process. Once labor had begun, to get through the pain, I needed to focus all my energies on a single point of light, having the faith to make it through. Usually a slow, cautious person, I now had to move quickly and respond immediately to events that were moving at an ever-accelerating and dangerous pace.

Ben's botanical obsession was growing stronger and stronger. Whenever I stopped for a signal and Ben spotted a tree, he tried to get out of the car in pursuit of autumn leaves, with little regard for danger. Once I entered the freeway, he stopped but after we exited, he began again.

In desperation, I remembered hearing of a child treatment facility that had recently opened in Grant's Pass. I had to stop for directions, then somehow get Ben down from a tree (no easy task since it had now begun to rain). Finally we reached the treatment center and, as we began to speak to an intake worker, Ben ran outside and began tearing leaves off the vegetation. The intake worker didn't immediately appreciate the extent of the problem.

"We only have a few temporary beds," she said, "and you need to go through your local health department. The process takes at least a month. Why don't you just give him a few leaves to hold as you drive back to Ashland?"

"You don't understand that he's in crisis," I told her. "Look what he's doing to your plants."

Now she began to become agitated, rushing outside.

"Stop that immediately," she told Ben, who ignored her. "If you don't stop immediately, I'll have to call the police."

When he continued to ignore her, she told us: "I'm sorry, I *will* have to call the police now to follow through. He needs to go to the emergency room."

A young police officer arrived, his voice calm, his face seeming angelic under the circumstances.

"You're going to have to go to the emergency room," he told Ben. "Should I take you or do you want to go with your mother and grandmother?"

"My mother," said Ben, quickly getting into the car.

"I'll lead the way," the officer told me. "Signal if you need any help."

I thanked him, trying to keep my presence of mind enough to follow him despite the rainstorm and having to drive through an unknown part of town. When we arrived at the hospital emergency room, a pattern began that would become only too familiar over the next few days.

After the initial assessment, the nurse told us: "We need to wait for the county mental health worker who'll do a psychiatric evaluation."

She arrived after a wait and, as it turned out, knew Sue, Ben's therapist. Then a straight-spoken but kindly emergency room doctor appeared.

"I want to try just giving him Lomotil first to calm him down. I'd rather not give him something stronger."

But the Lomotil failed to control Ben's impulses and he tried to run out of the emergency room towards some autumn trees. Two nurses held him down and, regretfully, the doctor gave him a shot of Haldol, which soon put him to sleep.

"Is there any way he could stay overnight?" we asked.

"All we have is a concrete room, and I wouldn't want to put him in there."

The rain had grown even stronger and I didn't think it was wise to try to drive back to Ashland in the dark. The nurses helped carry Ben into the car and we drove off, deciding to stay in a motel for the night.

"How'll we get him into the room?" I asked my mother. "He's too heavy for us to lift."

"We'll get help from the motel staff," my mother said, never losing her presence of mind.

We managed to get a room and a young man helped carry Ben inside, probably assuming he'd simply fallen asleep. Physically and psychologically exhausted, we sank into a deep sleep. Eight hours later, Ben awakened and immediately tried to run outside in pursuit of leaves.

"I'll pack if you can check out," I shouted to my mother and somehow managed to move fast enough to get Ben into the car with the suitcase.

But I had to immediately start driving—the minute I slowed down, Ben would try to leap out. My poor mother kept wheeling her suitcase around the parking lot in the rainstorm, trying to intersect with us. Finally, we were all in the car driving towards the freeway when I looked at the gas gauge.

"We don't have enough gas to make it back to Ashland," I said, having to choose between the lesser of two evils—risking an escape attempt when we stopped or running out of gas on the freeway in a storm.

I had removed Ben's shoes, hoping he wouldn't want to run barefoot in the cold rain. But, oblivious to the temperature, he made a dash for a tall birch, somehow managing to scramble up the wet bark. I paid for the gas and somehow managed to get him down from the tree and drive back to Ashland despite pouring rain and a windshield that kept fogging up.

I desperately need to decompress but no sooner had we arrived, then Ben tried to run out of the house and I realized we had to head back to an emergency room.

This time, we drove to the larger regional hospital, ironically, the place where Ben had been born. As I checked in, the clerk asked me: "Has he ever been here before?"

"He was born here," I said, a pang of anguish seizing me at the totally different emotions I was feeling during this second visit. But again, I had to focus on somehow marshalling my faculties and judgment to get us through the dark tunnel, having faith that there *would* be a way through.

This time, they immediately put Ben into a padded room with a magnetic lock, allowing me to stay with him while, as in Grant's Pass, they contacted a mental health worker for a psychiatric evaluation. Ben asked to use the restroom and we rang the bell to be let out. But as the door opened, Ben again made a dash for it. This time, four nurses grabbed him and without asking any questions, pinned him down and gave him a shot of Haldol. As a result, when the mental health worker arrived, Ben was unconscious.

"There really isn't much I can do," the worker said. "The psychiatric ward at the hospital only admits patients over 18."

"But what happens when he wakes up?" we demanded.

"You can always bring him back to the emergency room for another shot of Haldol," he answered.

This didn't seem like much of a solution but over our protests, they sent us back home, this time with a prescription for Haldol. Ben came to at 2.00 a.m., ate something and by morning, tried to run out of the house again.

"Call George," I said. "We need help."

Our friend George came over immediately, as well as bringing us bagels for breakfast.

"Now Ben, let's talk."

George, also a bilingual French/English speaker, has always had a good rapport with Ben. Talking worked for a while but then Ben tried to climb out a second-story window.

"Get some strapping tape," George shouted to me.

My hands trembling, I managed to find some.

"Now cut a piece about a foot long and help me get it around his wrists."

I followed his instructions, horrified at having to be an instrument in binding my child's hands and feet but needing to save his life.

"Take him to the emergency room at Ashland Hospital," he said. "Leave the tape on so they can understand the situation."

So we headed out to our third emergency room in three days, this time, to our local hospital; this proved to be a wise choice. As chance would have it (and a benefit of living in a small town), the emergency room doctor was the same person who had bought our car as we were leaving for France in 1991.

I recounted my story for the third time in three days, expecting to be told again that they would give Ben a shot of Haldol and send him home until the next outburst. But the doctor surprised me.

"This is ridiculous," he said. "You're going through a revolving door of emergency rooms. We have to do something about it. There's a child and adolescent psychiatric ward in Portland—we need to get Ben up there for proper treatment."

I watched in amazement as he began to make phone calls, wading through hospital and insurance company bureaucracy.

"He'll have to be seen by a psychiatrist so that'll mean transfer to the regional hospital," he told us.

A part of me groaned inwardly at the thought of a fourth emergency room in three days but at least we were making some forward progress.

Meanwhile, Ben had attempted to run outside again as soon as the strapping tape was cut; this time, rather than receiving another shot of Haldol, he was tied to a stretcher in restraints.

"He'll have to be transported by ambulance," the doctor said.

I tried to thank him for listening, for helping us find a way out but he modestly dismissed my compliments.

"I had the advantage of reading the reports from the previous emergency rooms," he said. "Anyone else would have done the same."

Once we arrived at the regional hospital, we again saw the same mental health worker from the previous day, now much more helpful in organizing Ben's transfer. I remembered something I'd heard in the first emergency room in Grant's Pass, and so I now said:

"I'd be afraid to drive him myself to Portland for a five-hour drive. I've heard about a service called Secure Transport."

From the time we reached Ashland Hospital to the time Secure Transport arrived, we had spent almost 12 hours in our third and fourth emergency rooms, with a brief return home to pack our suitcases for Portland. The hospital had given Ben a sedative, removed restraints and his shoes, then a very helpful French-Canadian woman (with whom Ben spoke French) rode in the back seat with him. I was allowed to go along, hardly able to stay awake until we reached the aptly named Providence Hospital in Portland.

"He's such a nice kid," the driver said. "I can't believe he arrived at the hospital in restraints."

At 2.00 a.m. I had to do an assessment, trying to sound as coherent as possible to the night nurse. Then Ben was taken to a room and I was able to stay in another part of the hospital, formerly quarters for the sisters. At 2.30 a.m., my simple room seemed palatial and though I'm Jewish, I felt protected by the crucifix over the bed. For the first time in many months, I was able to sink into a profound sleep, knowing my child was safe.

FOR DAYS, I didn't even have the strength to leave the hospital walls. After the overwhelming, continuous stress, all I could do was stay in this safe haven, visiting Ben during visiting hours, beginning to recover a little of my energy and equilibrium. But I realized Ben's stay would only be short term, and that I would need to use some of my respite to plan out the next steps, to move forward, never to fall back again into the dark tunnel from which we were just tentatively beginning to emerge.

As has often happened in my life, I began to receive the same message from two different directions. The first came from Ben's wonderful psychiatrist during a discussion of possible resources for Ben post-hospitalization.

"I have to be honest with you," he said, "if you stay in Oregon, you'll be reinventing the wheel. The resources Ben needs aren't here."

I felt both appreciative and surprised by his honesty.

"What do you recommend then?" I asked.

"We've sent a number of kids down to Los Angeles to the UCLA Neuropsychiatric Institute."

My first reaction was to burst out laughing. "For years I've avoided Los Angeles," I said. "I spent the first 17 years of my life vowing never to return to live there, leaving for Berkeley in my freshman year. But I'm willing to keep an open mind to help Ben."

"The first thing you need to do is find out if your insurance benefits will transfer and if NPI has any openings."

As it turned out, the insurance company was closed for the Thanksgiving holiday, so I had a day to contemplate this next possible move. As chance or sychronicity would have it, another event, coming from a somewhat unlikely direction, would help me perceive the way ahead clearly. My cousin, who lives in Portland, had invited me and Greg for Thanksgiving dinner.

It was a welcome relief from everything I had been through to spend a normal evening celebrating a joyous occasion. She had invited another family and the mother, finding out I lived in Ashland, asked me what had brought me to Portland. I hesitated, my usual tendency being not to bother others with my own life situation, especially on a holiday. But something compelled me to tell the full reason:

"Our son went into crisis and is in the child psychiatric facility at Providence Hospital. They're not sure if he has Asperger's Syndrome or obsessive compulsive disorder."

Astonished by my own boldness, I was even more astonished by her response:

"We're very familiar with the child and adolescent facility; our children have been through a number of times for OCD. That's why I started the Oregon Family Support Network, to help parents in similar situations."

"I can't believe this," I said. "I was afraid of ruining everyone's Thanksgiving dinner by talking about our family's problems."

"Not at all," said the daughter. "Most of our dinner conversations are about OCD and related topics."

Before the evening was up, the mother had given me the names of two families in the network, one with a child with OCD, the other with an Asperger's child. In the next couple days, I contacted them. The Asperger's Syndrome mother told me:

"The best book on the subject is by Dr. Tony Attwood and Oasis is a helpful website."

The OCD mother did something that I found incredibly moving and will never forget.

"Our son went down to UCLA NPI and I'd be more than happy to share information and resources with you. I'll be right over to meet you at Providence."

When I met her in the hospital lobby, she immediately gave me a warm hug.

"I know exactly what you're going through. We've been there."

Though I'm not usually the sort of person who shows her emotions in public, I burst into tears. For so long, with very few exceptions, I'd felt so alone, and that I had to present a strong façade simply to make it through each day so no one understood what I was going through on an emotional level.

"The first thing you'll want to get," she told me, "is a little notebook where you put all the UCLA phone numbers. You'll find yourself using them over and over again."

Following her advice, I reserved a little green notebook I'd bought in France, which would be in shreds three years later from so much use. This was only one of the practical tips she gave me. In a few short hours, she provided me with a virtual road map of how to navigate through the complexities of UCLA NPI. I left with a determination to get Ben down there no matter how difficult the process.

I also felt deeply emotionally nourished by the fact she had taken the time to share her experience as a person further along the road. Again, I thought of the difficulty of directly repaying someone, of how all one can do is to help someone else at the beginning of the road. I have tried to do this ever since. No matter how complicated my life is, I am always ready to speak to anyone about Asperger's Syndrome and my experience.

I redoubled my efforts to wade through the red tape to get Ben into UCLA NPI. NPI was ready to accept him when I described going to four emergency rooms in three days. When I'd inquired months earlier about NPI, I'd been told there was a waiting list of several months. Now I realized the fast track in was through the emergency room—not a track I'd recommend.

The next matter was whether our insurance would cover the cost. I was told that NPI cost $1000 a day and that Ben needed at least a two-week stay. Our insurance covered ten days of hospitalization and we'd already used up a number of days at Providence. By the time the company was back in the office after Thanksgiving, I was told we only had four days of coverage left.

I'm usually a cautious person who does extensive research before taking even calculated risks. But this time, I knew I had to act quickly, trusting largely on my intuition and having faith that somehow, I would be able to come up with a way to fund the additional days that Ben needed. I phoned to have him admitted the following day.

The next challenge was to make sure he would be safe on the journey down, this time by plane. I was able to arrange for the same French-Canadian woman, from Secure Transport, to accompany us. We flew to LA and got Ben checked into NPI. A journey which had begun by taking us north to Portland now brought us south to California without us having had a chance to return to our home in Ashland.

I arrived in California with my winter clothes from Oregon, to temperatures that felt balmy in comparison. Just as I had had my first sound night's sleep in several months at Providence Hospital, so did I fall gratefully into bed in my childhood bedroom. For the first time in years, I felt protected, warm, supported. I could begin to rest up and heal while my child began his healing at UCLA NPI. The Ashland chapter in Ben's life was coming to an end as a new Los Angeles chapter was beginning in my life.

Chapter Seven

Shortly after my arrival in Los Angeles, I had a dream about fragmentation that seemed to speak of both present and future. In the dream, I stood in my mother's kitchen in LA. Suddenly I noticed my Ashland teapot on a top shelf. As I examined it more closely, I realized it was in fragments, held together only by strands of algae, but still retaining its form.

The dream held an affect both of sadness (at the fragmentation of my teapot) and wonder that it still managed to hold together by strands of a natural substance. As I began to analyze the dream, I realized it continued the theme of the fragmentation of my Ashland life, the wrenching away of the family unit from our home. The significance of the algae would only reveal itself to me two and a half years later. As I worked through this dream with Sue by phone, she commented:

"Sometimes things need to fragment in order to be made whole again."

My carefully constructed life in my beloved Ashland had fragmented, replaced by the long-dreaded, long-avoided city of my birth. Suddenly, LA—which had always represented my past, a place I could escape from after brief vacations—had become my present. Ashland, my house, friends, normal activities, had overnight become my past.

With Ben at NPI for two weeks as an inpatient, for the first time in years I had a chance to fully acknowledge my own feelings rather than being in a constant state of alert, moving from crisis to crisis. My overwhelming feeling, once I began to get over my tremendous exhaustion, was one of disorientation. I felt relieved and protected sleeping in my blue childhood bedroom, amidst familiar surroundings, driving past landmarks I had known for decades. But I also felt besieged by a dual perspective. Emotions from my childhood kept rushing past me as I tried to begin to deal with Los Angeles of the present.

I felt the sadness of being cut off from my Ashland support network, having little to reconnect with on a human level after an absence of so many years. I also knew I had only a two-week window in which to figure out the next step. The image came to me of jumping from one slippery stone to the next over tumultuous waters, never knowing when I would again reach solid ground. I felt we had been carried to LA by a very swift current. Once entered, one could only proceed onward. Though I couldn't yet see all the steps ahead, I knew, for now, there would be no going back to Ashland except for brief visits.

As it turned out, I wouldn't see my home again until March of the following year. And the whole meaning of home was shifting by returning to my childhood house. I had left Oregon with only my winter clothes and now found myself in the perpetual spring of California.

One of the only bridges that carried me through this transition was the music of singer/songwriter Bill Staines. We'd become acquainted with Bill Staines' music since 1996.

"October 11, 1996," Ben of the photographic memory would tell me five years later, almost to the day.

"You have to go hear this guy," our folk music friend had told us back then in Ashland. "He's the one who wrote 'A Place in the Choir.'"

I went, more for the then ten-year-old Ben, with his growing interest in playing guitar and folk music, than for myself. Before the concert, I bought Ben a copy of Bill's songbook, *Music to Me.*

Ben followed along avidly throughout the concert, his absolute pitch and innate musical ability coming into play. But his as yet undiagnosed Asperger's Syndrome also came into play. He began to become agitated, speaking to me in a loud stage whisper.

"Why isn't he singing the songs in the same order as the book?" he asked.

I tried to put off answering his question until later. As the daughter of a musician, I was raised never to speak during an artist's performance. But Ben persisted.

"And why is he singing songs that aren't in the book?"

As Ben's questions became louder and more persistent, I saw no other course than to leave, which we did shortly. Fortunately, we had also bought Bill's latest recording, *Going to the West*, which we were able to hear numerous times during the following year. We liked it so much we bought copies for friends in France. The next summer, as we were driving to the international Celtic music festival in Lorient, Brittany, Ben and his friends, Celine and Aurore, happily sang the chorus of "I'm Going to the West" which I will always hear in my mind in a French accent.

With his double dose of obsessiveness (musical giftedness plus Asperger's Syndrome), Ben began tracking down every single song Bill had ever written and/or recorded. We even called Folk Legacy Records in search of Bill's first songbook, now out of print.

"Let me check in the basement," said the helpful owner of Folk Legacy and, sure enough, she came up with what was probably the last copy in the US of *If I Were a Word, Then I'd Be a Song.*

As I listened to the results of Ben's research, little by little, I found myself being drawn into the world of Bill's music. I began studying the songs with our music teacher, Dave. In his highly intuitive way, Ben began "prescribing" songs for me to learn. Though social norms and human emotions sometimes baffle Ben, he is perfectly at home in the realm of advanced philosophical speculation and the intricacies of guitar technique. He figured out which songs would suit me.

"I think you should learn 'Prairie Song,'" he told me.

I did and found myself moved not only by words and music but also by the deeper theme of an intuitive wisdom which expresses itself over time. Between 1996 and 1998, I was especially attracted by what Ben would term "Bill's spiritual songs," such as "Crossing the Water" and "Bridges."

During the years when our family life grew more and more stressful, I would sing Bill's spiritual songs as a light through our darkness. One song I kept singing in November 1998 was "Going Back Where the Wheat Fields Wave" (originally "prescribed" for me by Ben) by Bill Staines and Logan English. Logan English is deceased and Bill has published the song. The words: "I packed my home up in my suitcase/And sailed off in the air" kept going through my mind.

In heading north to Portland to Providence Hospital, though we didn't realize it at the time, we *had* "packed our home up in our suitcase." Without having a chance to return home to Ashland, we had "sailed off in the air," to UCLA NPI.

At NPI, they allowed Ben to bring a tape recorder and cassettes into the hospital, and he chose the songs of Bill Staines. One night during visiting hours, I brought in a backpack guitar, and we sang "Crossing the Water" and "Down the Road." I hadn't realized our voices were carrying beyond Ben's room but later one of the staff came by.

"Thank you so much for bringing light into this place," he told us. "Those songs were so beautiful."

I thanked him, wishing in retrospect I'd told him who wrote the songs, that we were only acting as channels for Bill Staines' music. I began to understand that the healing power of the songs extended beyond us into others' lives as well.

In the months that followed, I would learn a great deal about Asperger's Syndrome, of how to deal better with Ben's gifts and challenges. And I was also learning about my personal journey as well. When I first sang "Down the Road," I had to take Bill's words on faith, that there *would* truly be "another song, another friend, another day" worth the singing, knowing, living, down the road.

AFTER MY INITIAL disorientation at finding myself back in LA, I was faced with my own choice about healing. Either I could stay stuck in my hate/hate childhood relationship with the city, feeling angry and trapped, or I could begin to look at the landscape from a different perspective. In a way, I see a parallel with having an unusual child—either one can bemoan the lack of guidebooks or move ahead to map out the unknown territory.

I chose the latter course and, as I soon discovered, maps would prove to be a very apt metaphor for the process, both for myself and Ben.

One reason I had never wanted to return to LA involved my fear of driving. Whereas some kids are extremely eager to learn to drive, I dreaded the prospect. Part of my fear may have stemmed from a childhood accident where our car went off the road at Inspiration Point at Yosemite, just missing falling over the incline. Also, trying to learn to ride a bike as a child, I didn't know how to use the footbrakes, and had to jump off the bike just before it went over the hills. Somehow, at age 18, I managed to pass my driving test with a few lessons but I still wasn't comfortable driving.

In Berkeley I had no need of a car, and could reach my classes and many fascinating places easily accessible by walking. After my Junior Year in France, I got a summer job in a French restaurant in LA that required night driving. With great trepidation, I memorized the route between the restaurant and my parents' home. I felt extremely proud of myself on my first attempt soloing at night, only realizing later, to my horror, I had driven the entire distance without putting on my lights. Apart from this one route, I continued to be terrified to drive anywhere in LA.

To Greg's credit, he helped me overcome my fear in Seattle by starting me off in parking lots until I grew comfortable with the car's mechanism (plus also learning stick shift). I drove a little in Seattle, Portland, Hawaii, but found Sevilla a relief by being able to rely on walking and public transportation. Only on the small scale of Ashland did I begin to feel self-confident and able to deviate from planned routes, adjusting to the presence of other cars and even venturing out onto the freeways in Oregon. I was learning "the art of improvisation," becoming able to depart from the "written score," not having to conform to a perfectionist model that had previously caused performance anxiety.

But transferring driving skills from a small town to a huge metropolis on the scale of LA was highly daunting. When it became apparent our stay in LA would extend beyond Ben's time at NPI, my mother said: "You'll need a car down here as soon as possible."

I'd left my car like my entire previous life in Ashland and, as it turned out, wouldn't be able to get back there until the following March. So we rented a little red car I nicknamed "roadster" in honor of Nancy Drew's car, probably to give myself more courage like the fearless girl detective. On previous visits, Greg had done most of the driving. The only route I had dared attempt was heading downhill from the Santa Monica Mountains, turning right on San Vicente, then proceeding west until I reached the ocean (my love of the ocean overcoming my fear of driving).

Now I found myself in a situation where I needed to get to NPI daily to visit Ben. I built up my self-confidence by exploring streets in ever-widening concentric circles in Santa Monica. Eventually, I extended my explorations to visiting favorite sites from my childhood.

As a non-driver with an undeveloped sense of direction during most of my previous residence in LA, I had little idea of how to find my way from point A to point B. Another part of my problem involved motion sickness during which I had to concentrate on the center yellow line rather than paying attention to routes and street signs. Though I always enjoyed traveling and family outings, I had little idea of how we arrived at our destinations.

As I gradually extended my concentric circles to venture farther and farther into the metropolitan area, one of the first places I chose to visit was the Farmer's Market, fairly close to my first childhood home in West Hollywood. With a certain amount of trepidation, I mapped out my route along surface streets (even now, the LA freeways still remain a challenge). To my amazement, I managed to find my way there with no wrong turns.

Now, for the first time in my life, I could see a logical progression, making my way through various parts of the city, understanding how one neighborhood led into another. Streets which I had previously recognized as the "May Company Wilshire Street" now took on their proper names of "Fairfax Avenue." As I drove through regions, landmarks I'd known since childhood, memories from the late 1940s and 1950s returned to me.

I remembered my mother taking us to the tearoom at the May Company Wilshire in an attempt to teach us ladylike behavior (fortunately this was not totally successful since, without some unladylike qualities, I never would have made it through the difficult years with few resources for Ben). The Art Deco architecture of the building had always fascinated me; it seemed like a secular temple of fine arts. I loved the pneumatic tubes through which the salespeople sent messages from floor to floor as well as the excitement of seeing the picture on the bottom of your plate if you ate all of your food.

One criticism of the city is that the landscape changes every few weeks as buildings are torn down with little consideration for historic preservation. May Company Wilshire, however, *has* been preserved now as a real temple of the fine arts, becoming part of the LA County Art Museum.

The Farmers' Market, I was delighted to discover, had changed little since my childhood so I was able to begin to orient myself with a familiar landmark after the chaotic disorientation of the past several months. Even the donut shop, always one of our childhood favorites, had changed in name only (from "Arnold's" to "Bob's"). Little by little, the feeling of overlapping realities, a present-day landscape overshadowed by memories from decades ago, began to merge into a single perspective. I was at least becoming comfortable driving around a city where I had never felt comfortable before, beginning to become grounded.

As has happened innumerable times since Ben's birth, developments in our lives often follow a parallel, complementary course. As I became more proficient in navigating my way around Los Angeles, working from the familiar childhood landmarks to the unknown, Ben developed a passion for maps.

In the interim between the end of his time at NPI and beginning a new educational placement, he had suddenly taken to studying Thomas Guides assiduously. With his unusual learning style and photographic memory, he quickly amassed vast amounts of data. A few months into the process, while we were driving around LA, he suddenly announced, totally from memory: "We're on page 632 of the LA Thomas Guide." Here, now, was another gift which might not have emerged had we not moved to a larger metropolitan area.

Soon we were making frequent field-trips to the UCLA Map Library as well as the California Map and Travel Store, with Ben searching out more and more obscure maps, including ones showing freeway overpasses and underpasses.

As Ben's questions grew more and more detailed, a map clerk suggested: "Where you really need to go is Mecca" (i.e., the corporate headquarters of Thomas Brothers Maps).

As luck would have it, I managed to call Thomas Brothers Maps the day before their giant camera, used for decades to prepare the guides, would be taken apart. Unlike my map fanatic brother, Bob, who learned to read by memorizing highway signs, I was never interested in maps as a child. Consequently, as noted above, I spent much of my childhood being lost. Only at age 19, on a visit to New York and determined to find my way to the UN, did I succeed in following a map to my destination.

I contacted someone who worked for the Educational Foundation. "We used to give tours," she explained to me, "but since the company was sold, we stopped. The camera's due to be dismantled tomorrow."

"Too bad," I said, telling her about Ben's passion for Thomas Guides.

She thought for a moment. "I'll be here until midnight," she said. "I don't usually do this but if you can get your son down here, I'll give him a personalized tour."

She gave me directions, telling me to have Ben search out the route on his LA/Orange County Thomas Guide (part of his growing collection). Later that night, we found ourselves at "Mecca," entering the foundation's archives. Eschewing polite formalities, Ben demanded:

"Where's Kern County?"

"In this row," our guide told him, "we have editions going back to 1981."

With Ben happily absorbed in one of the guides he'd been unable to find at the UCLA Map Library, I wondered if we'd ever be able to wrest him away long enough to tour the plant. Eventually however, we entered the high-ceilinged cavern where Thomas Guides had been produced for years. Huge piles of finished guides—Contra Costa, LA, geographical locations spanning the state—reached skyward.

"We really should start at the beginning," our guide said. "You should hear it in here when the presses and collators are operating."

Thinking of Ben's hypersensitivity to sound, we secretly felt glad to be touring the plant after hours. I found my excitement growing as we neared the primal source.

"This is how they start out," she said, picking up an uncut set of four pages. "Then here's the assembly line for collating and cutting."

We examined the hole puncher, the familiar Thomas Guide bindings. Then we arrived at a fenced-off area.

"We could get through to the camera this way," she said, "but it looks like it's locked."

We serpentined through corridors which led to an alternative route to the camera.

"It came off a World War II destroyer," she told us. "Here's where they put the mylar plate of an entire page to photograph."

She showed us an enormous page of a Thomas Guide. This was part of the production method that had been used for decades, now to be replaced by computerized methods. She described how she had tried to find a museum home for the camera in limited time, but none had materialized. We tried to brainstorm possible solutions, even knowing time had run out. Ben, true to form, was scrupulously examining giant wall maps, memorizing every detail according to the unique pathways of his brain.

I found myself experiencing a variety of emotions—sadness at seeing a piece of history vanish, and at the changes in LA since my childhood—joy in Ben's exhilaration at scrutinizing a plethora of maps. Watching Ben, I thought of how geographical relationships, which have sometimes been laborious for me because of my lack of experience, are grasped instantaneously by him though social relationships and some emotions remain difficult terrain for him.

We left, arms full of maps including an enormous LA County wall map and a recent Portland Guide. One thing our guide said echoes through my mind:

"Maps shape our view of reality."

She described how children assume that Alaska and Hawaii are islands because that's how they appear on maps, separate from the contiguous states. I realized that this second, unexpected residence in LA and Ben's strong interests and curious challenges had plunged me into the world of map making. I welcomed the chance of acquiring new tools as I begin to remake my own personal map.

I also thought of Ben's interest in maps as a fitting metaphor for an Asperger's person who tries to make sense of a world where, so often, the bridges and connections seem not to be there.

Chapter Eight

I had already begun charting my own inner map the year before
leaving Ashland. Sue and I would talk frequently by phone,
problem-solving Ben's crises. I would feel much calmer after our
conversations and in the late spring of 1997 I decided to take the
plunge and begin therapy with her for myself.

At my first session, I decided to try the Jungian sand tray. But
instead of using the miniature figurines, I immersed my hands in the
sand. Suddenly, I was back on a beach in France 1967, re-experiencing
emotions long forgotten.

Sue commented a few sessions later:

"Susan is a vast unexplored territory."

My commitment to begin to map out that inner territory continued
even after the tumultuous journey to Los Angeles. Just as Ben kept on
doing his lessons with Dave, now by phone, so did I begin phone
sessions with Sue. My dreams, always intense, were growing progres-
sively stronger and eventually, I found Laurie, a dream therapist in Los
Angeles, to supplement my sessions with Sue. Now I began to map out
the even more alien territory of my dreams, which, at times, seemed to
reach into the prophetic.

About a week before the crisis that precipitated our journey to LA, I had an extremely powerful dream. People with Asperger's Syndrome receive information through different channels; in the same way, I believe dreams can provide us with an alternative form of knowledge, sometimes not bound to customary limits of time and space. Though a dream may appear opaque at the time, often it may provide a parallel narrative of a developing process, a catalyst in my life, just as Ben continues to be.

My last strong dream before the crisis took place in the narrow hallway of our Ashland house. In the dream, three gray elephants stood in the hallway, two adult ones and a juvenile. A voice told me:

"The little one is cute but he will grow."

The unstated implication was that the already overly small space couldn't possibly contain three adult-sized elephants. Meanwhile, I noticed a physically disabled woman named "Mary Cunningham" crammed into an extremely tight cupboard at the end of the hallway. I knew, somehow, she was a Jungian analyst.

Then a (previously non-existent) staircase leading from the basement appeared in the middle of the living room. Two women were coming up the staircase. They looked pointedly at me and asked:

"Are you a follower of the ideas of C.G. Jung?"

Before I had a chance to answer, the dream ended. I now realize the dream predicted the fragmentation of our household in Ashland. The three gray elephants represented the aspect of our family that had run out of space (and resources) in Ashland and that if the baby elephant, Ben, were to grow, he would need more space. I also see the physically disabled Jungian psychologist, cramped into too small a space, as an aspect of myself. I could see a part of myself who had dealt for too long with a highly difficult situation with extremely limited resources and whose own development had been crippled in the process.

The two women coming up the staircase suggest a direction from which future explorations could come—by examining issues long stored in the basement (i.e. the unconscious), new insights would arise. I see their question about being a follower of Jung as an invitation to begin the inner journey, to bring ideas hitherto relegated to the darkness of "the basement" into the light of the "living room" (i.e. the conscious part of my life, also conveying the idea of "room" or space).

Finding Laurie, the LA dream therapist, involved not only a journey into new territory but the first time in many years searching out a resource for myself rather than Ben. At the initial meeting of the dream group, I was faced with an unexpected crossroads. As I began narrating the dream I'd brought in, I suddenly realized that fully describing the dream would reveal very personal emotional struggles. Though I have been a private person for most of my life, I knew that if I censored the dream, I would close myself off from the potential benefits of the group, not doing justice to myself or to the dream.

After I had finished, Laurie and the other members were silent. Then she spoke:

"Are you aware of what the dream is saying about your situation?"

"Yes," I said, feeling a tremendous sense of relief, finally breaking a vow of silence, which had oppressed me for decades.

In the group, then in private sessions, I began to map out my journey, at first in the safer territory known as "thought experiment." Later, I would extend my explorations into the world of action, radically changing the path of my life. By respecting my dreams and taking them seriously, energies long dormant began to reawaken, energies I would need both for my own development and to help guide Ben.

My dream work with Laurie also led to an unexpected resource for Ben. This time, a resource I'd located for myself led back to him. Along with maps, Ben was developing an avid interest in National Geographic animal videos. When Laurie mentioned her husband was a filmmaker, I asked:

"What sorts of films does he make?"

"Mostly documentaries like National Geographic animal videos."

Her husband Sasha kindly agreed to be interviewed by Ben. Accompanying him, I myself learned some fascinating behind the scenes details about filming beaver behavior, etc.

An unexpected gift of Ben's Asperger's Syndrome and his intense interests is the opportunity to expand my own educational horizons.

Through him, I learn about myriad subjects that never would have otherwise crossed my intellectual field of vision. His research into the work of Woody Guthrie, for example, led to the discovery of hitherto unpublished work at the Smithsonian and an invitation by the curator to visit in person the next time we happen to be in Washington, DC.

Dream therapy helped expand the psychological boundaries of my inner journey. My initial decision that none of the dream material would be "off limits" began to extend into my waking life as well. The image of "closed cities" in the former Soviet Union comes to mind, cities closed to foreigners because of military security, nuclear secrets etc. On a trip to the former Soviet Union, I was unable to visit my grandfather's birthplace of Dneprpetrovsk (now Ekaterineslav) because it was then a "closed city." Though tensions in numerous areas of my life had been building for years, I had never crossed the border into "forbidden territory." Yet somehow, I had known for years that, if I ever returned to Los Angeles, my life would change radically.

I don't know how long it would have taken me to step over the border into awareness of what was really going on had it not been for Dr. A. She entered our lives as an in-home behavioral psychologist who came for weekly visits to work on family issues. Though young enough to have been our daughter, Dr. A. soon showed the wisdom and compassion of an old soul.

A lovely, intelligent young person with a good sense of humor, Dr. A. quickly began to develop an excellent rapport with Ben. From her, we learned how to find a halfway ground with him, a middle way between the extremes of Ben's Asperger's and the neurotypical extremes, both sometimes exhibiting their own rigidity. I had been concentrating for so long on finding resources for Ben, while dealing with his day-to-day challenges with limited help, that I had given little thought to my own life's path.

As often happens in families with Asperger's children, the stress of dealing with the day-to-day situations—especially when resources are limited—and the differences in approaches even among professionals were putting our marriage under strain. From my own experience, I think it's imperative to address such marital pressures directly and at an early stage. Even if couples' therapy leads to separation, both parents can develop a good relationship as friends and bring their respective strengths to their Asperger's child as co-parents.

Dr. A. agreed to take on the additional role of couple's therapist and in the summer we began sessions. Somehow, I assumed at the beginning that the end result of the therapy would be that our problems were worked out and marriage back on track with a firmer foundation. At the time it never occurred to me that the ultimate result might be the decision to separate. It also hadn't occurred to me that all parties have to be ready to work through much anger, pain, and sadness.

I learned that it's all right for everyone to express a full range of emotions in order to reach a level of understanding that will enable both parents to work together in the best interest of their child, as well as gaining more insight into their own psyches and life paths.

When I realized we were heading towards separation, at first I felt cast into unknown territory, bereft of familiar landmarks, back in tumultuous waters with land nowhere in sight. Again, the dream of fragmentation was being made manifest in my life.

Throughout all the changes of the previous 30 years—geographical, living abroad, exploring our careers, having a child—I had seen our relationship as a supportive protective matrix. Even as more and more problems and stresses surfaced, I never questioned the structure itself, somehow believing it would remain intact even once couple's therapy began.

By allowing myself to perceive and acknowledge the entire spectrum of emotions for both of us, I could begin to map out my position in the marital landscape and movement finally became possible. I now understood that we had left the territory of "if" for the territory of "when."

"When" came almost two years later. I needed to try to adjust to this new landscape, to begin to plan out a life alone I'd never thought I'd have to envisage.

A few months before our actual separation, I had a dream of "Alternative Susan." In the dream, I find some green pages from a little

French notebook. One side of each page is in my handwriting describing the influence of Cinderella on my life. On the other side, in pencil, someone else has written the story of "Alternative Susan."

I begin reading how Alternative Susan was a rock star in Ashland in 1967, then went on a tour with her band to Tanzania, which ended badly. As I'm reading, her story changes to photographic images printed on fabric (a loose dress with an orange background). I put on the dress, then see a gray-haired woman, whom I realize is the author of the story, giving a speech. She's ready to introduce Alternative Susan, to present her with an award. She looks in my direction.

"But I'm not Alternative Susan," I protest; no one believes me.

Later, a young woman comes up to me and says: "It's too bad Susan no longer works for Harry."

"Susan who?" I ask.

"Susan Rubinyi," she answers.

"But I've never worked for Harry. You must mean Alternative Susan."

She nods but I can tell she doesn't believe me either.

When I brought this dream to Laurie, she pointed out:

"But you *are* Alternative Susan as well."

As I thought about this, I realized I had spent so much time and energy locating creative resources for Ben that for a long time many aspects of my own life had lain dormant, almost forgotten. Because of Ben's educational complexities, my dormancy period had lasted far longer than do most parents', with no end in sight. But my unconscious, in the form of this dream, was telling me it was time for Alternative Susan to awaken. I needed to begin to act now rather than waiting for the perfect time and circumstances.

Parts of the dream immediately made sense—the little green French notebook reflecting the continuing importance of both French and writing for me. And the Cinderella story has literally played a highly significant role in my life.

When I was very young, my parents taped our family doing a dramatic rendition of Cinderella. I was cast in the title role, my sister as one of the wicked stepsisters. Our friend, totally out of character, played the other wicked stepsister. My mother was the Fairy God-mother, my father, the handsome prince (and the chimes at midnight and other pianistic sound effects).

A lot has been written about the negative influences on girls of the Cinderella story—passivity, suffering in silence, waiting to be rescued by the handsome prince. The story can also be approached from an alternative direction, however: the discovery and acknowledgement of hidden worth. I see the dream's juxtaposition of Cinderella and Alternative Susan as two aspects of the same person. Though much of Alternative Susan had gone underground for years, she was re-emerging as I prepared for life on my own.

I knew her to be a person of light and color, unafraid to assert herself as she explored over a very expansive territory. I sensed she was also comfortable being fully herself which included being Jewish. I was returning to the crossroads I had left, the interrupted journey. But at this point, my life had been tempered and enriched by having to deal with the challenges and gifts of a child with Asperger's Syndrome. As I moved forward into this new territory, I would need to use this wisdom both for my own sake and for Ben's.

Chapter Nine

For a long time I had thought linearly: "Once Ben's education is in place, I can begin to figure out the financial picture, find a place to live, then separate." But when the decision to separate actually came, I proceeded quite differently. I knew I had to act quickly and decisively, while the window was open. Not knowing where Ben and I would live nor how we would keep our heads above water financially, I moved all of our belongings out of my mother's house into a storage locker and headed north for a few weeks in Ashland.

On my return, I had to face another of my fears. Though I had looked for housing independently in Berkeley, then with Greg in a myriad other places, I had never tried to find a place to stay in LA. I had always landed back in my mother's house. I found the immense size of the *LA Times* classified ads overwhelming. But, taking a deep breath, I started searching through listings in various parts of the city. Expecting the process to take several weeks, I decided to look for a month's rental for me and Ben while I searched for something longer term.

"Might as well be in a place I enjoy," I thought, and I knew immediately I'd look by the ocean.

I found an ad for temporary rentals that said: "Steps from the beach." Though this particular apartment turned out to be beyond our means, we were able to find a larger, less expensive one nearby. As things turned out, the apartment was also available long term and, a week after our search began, it had ended.

Though I hadn't started any utility accounts in almost 20 years, fortunately, one of the Ashland accounts was in my name so I had established credit. The one aspect I hadn't thought through was the challenge of convincing a person with Asperger's Syndrome, who disliked change, to spend the first night in a totally new environment minus one family member.

I was so exhausted from the search, the move, the separation, I wanted nothing more than to relax in our new abode. Ben said nothing until we'd moved everything in, then announced:

"I don't want to stay in this apartment."

Though I was ready to blow up at this point, I knew from Dr. A.'s teaching that if I did so Ben would only focus on my affect rather than the content of what I was saying. As *his* affect and tone began to rise, fearful of being evicted on the first night, I said:

"Let's go out for a drive."

I knew how important beginnings are for people with Asperger's Syndrome, setting up a template for what follows. If Ben could agree to spend the first night in the new apartment, we'd be home free. Being able to see the apartment as a positive alternative could help overcome his resistance to change. As I drove along Wilshire Boulevard, he began to calm down.

"Can't we go back to Grandma's?" he asked.

"No, we've stayed there for two years."

"Then what about a motel?"

I almost said: "Too expensive" when a thought occurred to me. Ben, himself, had provided a possible solution.

"OK," I said, "let's look at one."

I stopped at an old, somewhat dilapidated motel and we asked to see a room, which Ben looked at critically.

"Thank you," I told the clerk. "My son and I'll talk this over."

In the car Ben asked: "Where was the bathtub?"

"There wasn't one, only a shower."

"But I can't go to sleep without a bath."

He thought for a moment, then said: "The apartment has a bath, doesn't it?"

I nodded, keeping my affect low but feeling a great sense of relief. We returned to the apartment. I unlocked the door but it refused to open.

"Oh no," I thought. "Here Ben's finally ready to stay in the apartment and we can't get in."

But having come this far, I wasn't giving up. As a last resort, I turned the key a little more and gave the door a push and it opened. Then, like on the night we had finally reached Providence Hospital in Portland, I sank into a deep sleep, having crossed the threshold.

SOMEHOW, IT HADN'T occurred to me until after we moved into the ocean apartment that Ben had also changed school districts. This would eventually turn out to be fortuitous. Though numerous resources for Asperger's Syndrome existed in LA (a blessing after the paucity of Oregon resources), we still continued to struggle to find/create an educational program for Ben that addressed both his gifts and his challenges.

After leaving NPI, Ben had spent two years at a school for kids with Asperger's Syndrome. Initially things went fairly well, due in large part to a very creative aide (and part-time musician) and a sympathetic teacher and head psychologist. Ben would spend part of the time in class, part of the time at a nearby college library with the aide doing research. Things changed dramatically for the worse the second year when the aide was removed and Ben refused to even enter the classroom, spending most of his time in the hallway. By June of 2001, we were left with few alternatives besides going into mediation.

One bright spot, however, was Ben's appearance at the "Beatlefest," a gathering of Beatles' fans and musicians that Dave told us about.

"It would be great if Ben could try out for the Beatles Sound-Alike contest."

Though I, in this situation, would have felt paralyzed by performance anxiety, here the Asperger's characteristic of lack of concern for others' opinions served Ben well. Even last-minute technical foul-ups failed to faze him. Shortly before he was due to perform, he told me:

"While I was cuing up my back-up tape for 'Twist and Shout,' it broke. Is there any way of fixing it?"

"Not in five minutes," I said.

"OK," he said calmly. "I'll do 'I Saw Her Standing There,' instead."

I was astonished with how well Ben handled a musician's ultimate nightmare: having to change the program at the last minute to an unrehearsed number. But with his photographic and auditory memory, Ben always carries a huge catalogue of songs in his head. Note perfect, he performed as if he had been rehearsing this particular song for months. As he left the stage, another contestant told me:

"His playing is excellent and he has a very nice voice."

Later, though he had never played with a band before, he joined right in with "Arthur," doing vocals and guitar for "Twist and Shout," "Paperback Writer," and "One After 909."

Afterwards, a band member told Greg:

"Sometimes a shy little kid like this comes up to the mike and sounds just like Aretha Franklin or another professional."

Having studied not only Dave's musicality but also his polished manner with an audience, Ben related with great ease to the listeners and other band members. He had absorbed Dave's encyclopedic knowledge of the Beatles and gave a running commentary on each song's history, noting not only American releases but also British.

Later that night, as we listened to a Beatles tribute band, Ben spotted a group of bilingual Beatles fans sitting behind us.

"Habla español?" he asked.

When the answer was "un poco," he went on to Italian and some of the other languages he'd been learning with the same thoroughness and rapidity as he learned the Beatles' songs.

Whereas Ben disregards social conventions, I tend to be overly aware of them and felt somewhat uncomfortable, hoping the group felt like talking about their language (which turned out to be Tagalog from the Philippines). But as they left, one of them told Ben.

"I'm so proud of you and your enthusiasm for the Beatles," he said. "May you have a good life."

As the last chords faded, the young man's words lingered over us like a prayer.

But making the connection between Ben's growing musical gift and his educational program continued to be challenging. Ben's new district after our move wasn't sure what to do with him (and no program was instituted for a year). We were fortunate that regional center resources filled in. Since our return to LA, we'd been highly impressed with California's exemplary system of regional centers for people with developmental disabilities. Following the advice from the support group LA Families with Children with Asperger's, we contacted a regional center counselor early on.

"I might as well do your intake [assessment] over the phone," said Harry Brown-Hiegel. "What year were you born?"

When I told him he said, to my surprise, "A very good year."

"Why do you say that?"

"I was born in the same year."

I immediately liked Harry's sense of humor and would discover he also had a sharp intelligence and well-developed sense of social justice. Though, at times, we've had widely differing perspectives, we've always been able to discuss various possible approaches within a supportive context. While Santa Monica was puzzling over a direction, Harry filled in by funding several hours a week of a social/recreational aide who turned out to be an immensely creative person.

Christa had been the drama coach at an autism camp and had bought a plethora of talents to her work with Ben. In addition to her background in drama, she was intelligent, warm, friendly, and had a quality Dr. A. had pointed out as essential:

"You have to like Ben to be able to work with him."

Christa played a very important role in the continuing emergence of Ben's musical ability, in his first major public concert. The concert came about in part from the efforts of Ben's wonderful psychiatrist, Dr. Schmidt-Lackner, whose practice consists primarily of people with Asperger's Syndrome. Ben had been seeing her from the time he left NPI. We greatly enjoyed her sense of humor and sharp mind coupled with her highly pragmatic approach and amazing knowledge of Asperger's Syndrome resources.

During one session in 2001, Ben brought in his guitar and played and sang for her.

"I'll call the director of the Autism Society right away," she said, "and recommend that Ben perform at the next annual autism conference."

Christa helped us every step of the way, offering to meet us at the hotel. Preparing for Ben's first major concert resembled preparing for a European trip. Of a myriad contingencies, some proved to be totally unnecessary while others materialized which totally escape one's initial planning. Car filled with musical instruments, back-up tapes and patch cords, Ben and I headed for the conference headquarters. I tried not to pack my own "musical performance anxiety," part of my baggage, not Ben's.

Thanks to Ben's expert reading of the Thomas Guide, we found our way to Pasadena along surface streets. Christa and a friend were waiting for us, helping unpack Ben's equipment. As we pulled up, I asked Ben to turn his Beatles CD down while I spoke with the parking attendant. But the attendant started snapping his fingers to the rhythm and singing along.

"I love the Beatles," he told us. "I'd sing their songs in the Philippines."

While I checked in, he and Ben sang a few songs with guitar accompaniment in the lobby. Later, we met Fred from the United Autism Alliance for a tour of the theater where Ben would be performing the next day. Over the phone, Fred had asked me:

"Will I be able to carry on a conversation with Ben?"

"Certainly," I had assured him, "but it might be a somewhat unusual conversation."

Fred walked up. "Hi Ben, I'm Fred."

"Hi Fred," said Ben, "what's kicking?"

Within a few minutes, Ben had covered his interest in John Lennon and the Beatles, and a few of his social justice concerns like his belief in the potential of people with Asperger's Syndrome. Later, he did a run-through of his program, more to reassure me on the technical aspects than from a need to practice. I had been assigned the role of putting on his back-up tapes.

"I don't see how I can locate 'Ticket to Ride,' in time," I told him.

"Let's do 'Strawberry Fields,' instead," Ben proposed. "It's right on the other side."

Convinced we had the problem solved, I got a good night's sleep. The next day, Christa and her friend arrived to help with the instruments. Proudly wearing his Rubber Soul tee-shirt, Ben headed out. We got to the theater, which I'd visualized as devoid of people during the set-up time. But conference participants were already taking their seats.

"Hi," said a helpful staff member of the United Autism Alliance. "I'll help with the set-up. The sound person'll be here shortly."

I felt extremely grateful for her help, neither of us realizing she would have to manage transferring the sound system cord numerous times between the keyboard and Ben's electric acoustic guitar. When the set-up was almost complete, Fred asked:

"Who's going to do the intro?"

Here was one of those unplanned details that arrive from the periphery.

"Let's ask Ben," I said, hoping he'd choose Fred.

"Mom," he answered.

With no time to get nervous, I was on, words somehow coming to me. Then it was time to put on the first back-up tape. From "Hey Jude" on, Ben was in tune with his audience. Even through minor glitches like discovering that he and the back-up to "We Can Work It Out" were half a measure apart, he quickly "worked it out," getting back on track.

I actually managed to relax and enjoy his performance until we got to the tape change for "Strawberry Fields." What we thought we'd worked out the night before now became a logistical nightmare with "Tax Man" appearing where I expected "Strawberry Fields" to be. I was ready to skip it entirely, going on to the next number but Ben, without missing a beat, smoothly covered for me. While holding the audience's attention, he calmly instructed me on how to locate the song.

The rest of the concert proceeded without incident. Ben neatly tied in his social justice concerns with the Beatles' lyrics.

"People don't appreciate what these poor Asperger's kids go through, what gifts they have to offer the world."

The audience of autism/Asperger's professionals and parents applauded Ben's words. Afterwards, audience members flocked around Ben and his dream of being able to sign autographs was finally fulfilled.

"If he ever comes north, we'd love to have him perform," a teacher who worked at an autistic spectrum school told me.

I spoke with parents, school psychologists, and people involved in the music industry. Ben told me later he was asked if anyone was doing a film on him. Outside the theater, a couple talked with Ben.

"Are you Ben's mom?" the man asked me.

I nodded.

"Or should I say, his roadie?" the man joked.

I'd never heard the term before and found out it referred to a musician's road technicians. I laughed at the idea of applying "roadie" to as non-technical a person as myself.

It was an amazing feeling to see Ben handle being a positive center of attention on his own, for me to be able to relinquish my role as interpreter with the neurotypical world. Later that evening he told me:

"I'm so happy. I could feel the audience's good energies coming towards me."

I realized that just as this concert represented a part of Ben's healing and my own, of focusing on gifts rather than deficits, so did he send healing energies into the audience, communicating his joy through music. He gave them the gift of hope for nurturing the potential of their own children and the children they work with.

To quote a statement Ben wrote to hand out at the concert, people with Asperger's Syndrome: "have been down a lot of hard roads and have often been misunderstood. But underneath it all, they are good people with a lot of creative ideas. If only people could listen to their ideas, the world could be a better place."

Chapter Ten

So often with Ben, one door opening has led to another. In situations like these, it becomes highly important that parents develop the flexibility and determination to perceive and follow through on multiple alternatives. In the aftermath of Ben's success performing solo at the autism conference, Fred proposed another opportunity.

"In a few months, we're sponsoring a Walk on Autism in Griffith Park. It may attract as many as 10,000 people. Would Ben be interested in opening?"

"I'll ask him," I said, thinking of how intimidated I would have felt even performing for an audience of ten.

Again, Ben's lack of performance anxiety, related in part to his Asperger's Syndrome, came in handy.

"Sure," he answered without the slightest hesitation, "I'd love to perform."

True to form, Ben did an excellent job as the opening act.

Ben's performances for the Autism Society would lead us to Ben's next musical mentor after Dave, Guy Marshall. Guy was to help broaden Ben's musical experiences, leading him into a new direction: recording.

"I'll need a back-up CD for John Lennon's 'Imagine,'" Ben had told me, mentally going through the parts.

We had met Guy a few months before, attending the first session of his course on making your own four-track recording. Though Ben wasn't yet able to sit through an entire class, we liked Guy and I'd asked him if he'd ever do private lessons.

"I have my own recording studio," he told us.

Ben and Guy worked well together and the "Imagine" back-up CD added greatly to Ben's performance. Here, openness to a creative approach proved to be essential. Had we focused solely on the fact that Ben wasn't yet ready to sit through a class, we would have closed a door, missing out on a creative resource person who could help further Ben's musical and personal development.

The next two years would involve a series of mediations with the school district to try to create a program incorporating Ben's gifts and strengths as a way to address his challenges. Many school districts, for a variety of reasons including financial, and/or ignorance of the gifted side of the Asperger's dual exceptionality, will try to fit the child into an existing program, no matter how inappropriate. Ben was "offered," for example, a class where 16-year-olds were learning the days of the week.

For a year, he ended up with individual after-school lessons from one of the high school teachers. I was impressed with one project the teacher came up with.

"Ben learns a lot by asking questions," he said. "How about having him do a survey on the Third Street Promenade [a pedestrian mall]?"

Ben and I both liked this idea and the teacher and Ben worked up a set of survey questions. The questions ranged over a wide variety of Ben's current political concerns including opinions on the death penalty, public nudity and, interestingly enough, the question: "Do you consider yourself a spiritual person?"

The eclectic nature of the questions and Ben's interests belie the common stereotype of Asperger's people as having a very narrow focus. I would guess that sometimes the extreme depth to which they research a subject is sometimes mistaken for narrowness.

"Ben and I'll take the survey to City Hall first," said the teacher, "to see if he needs any kind of special permit."

I found this step to be a very creative, experiential way of teaching Ben about city government. Ben had a great time giving his survey to residents and tourists, reaching his goal of interviewing 100 people. The survey also helped him practice social interaction and conversational skills in a socially appropriate context. His bilingualism came in handy as well.

"We ran into a number of French tourists," the teacher told me, "and Ben interviewed them in French. They were astonished to meet an American kid who knew perfect French."

We had also arranged for Dave to come down to perform with Ben in what turned out to be a "standing room only" concert/conversation. Organizing Ben's concert exemplified the unwavering dedication parents of children with Asperger's Syndrome need to turn a creative idea into a reality. Though all parents can use such dedication, we are required, as well, to deal with the day-to-day fluctuations of the syndrome which often require a great deal of energy and finesse.

After I had already begun arranging for Dave to come down, assuming he and Ben could perform at the high school, Ben's teacher said:

"I'm afraid the concert's off because they can't use the high school."

Whenever I've been told something's impossible, my first response is to become even more determined to find another way around.

"Then we'll find another venue," I said.

After much research, many detours, I finally located a lovely historic church. Not only had the minister heard of Asperger's Syndrome, but once she found out that Dave directed the choir at the Ashland Methodist Church she said:

"That's great. You can get the Methodist Church rental discount."

Our cousin met with me during the planning stage. As I discussed various components, publicity etc., she immediately offered to help with a considerable number of tasks, then said something that few people have ever said before:

"What else can I do?"

I was speechless at first and very moved, having rarely met someone willing to volunteer beyond what was asked. Thanks to her and other people's help, we ended up with a standing room only crowd. Up until almost the last minute, my determination would be tested a number of times more as we struggled to overcome hurdles with the sound system, malfunctioning computers and fax machines, Dave's laryngitis, etc. I am eternally grateful to Greg for doing a last-minute run to make enough copies of the programs.

While I was preoccupied with all the nitty-gritty details, Ben remained calm, unfazed, totally lacking in performance anxiety. As the performance time neared, many philosophical questions crossed his mind. His conversational opener to Dave after we picked him up at the airport was:

"Tell me, Dave, have you ever thought about your first conscious memory?"

Later that evening, he asked a woman involved in the site recording:

"Tell me something, have you ever thought deeply about the meaning of life and why we're here on earth? Don't you think we should help one another create world peace?"

Later she told me: "Your son asks such interesting questions. He's really charming."

I greatly appreciated this reaction rather than "Why does your son ask such weird questions?"

Once the concert began, music alternated with words in that particular flowing synergy Dave's always had with Ben, eliciting a very deep level of music and thought. My role as organizer and "roadie" finished for now, I vowed to attempt to relax, regardless of what Ben might happen to say in public. Musically, he was in top form, his voice reflecting subtle nuances in the melodies I'd never noticed before.

"I've been down some long dark roads," Ben told the audience, in between songs, "including my two hospitalizations."

He certainly got their attention, then. As the concert continued, I could feel positive energies spread through the church and I felt truly grateful for having given birth to this child. After the concert, the audience burst forth with a standing ovation and people rushed up to congratulate me.

"But I wasn't up there performing," I said.

"You still deserve to be congratulated for making this possible."

I thought of all the obstacles Ben, as a person with Asperger's Syndrome, had overcome to be able to perform in public. I thought, as well, of the obstacles I had had to overcome to be fairly comfortable with his sometimes highly unconventional public comments.

In the true form of musicians, Dave and Ben went through their own critiques.

"Too bad I wasn't in my best voice with my laryngitis," said Dave.

"I only am tapping a small part of my potential," Ben commented later prophetically.

Once I got home, I collapsed on the bed in my clothes, unable to move; the evening's harmonies, audible and inaudible, continued to resonate through my dreams.

AS A RESULT of the concert, Ben received his first interview from a very nice British reporter for a local paper.

"I saw your flyer in the Co-op," she told me, "and I'd like to send a photographer over, then do a phone interview."

"Sure," I answered, wondering how Ben would respond to his first real interview. As with many other aspects of our journey, I had to rely on faith that he would be able to handle the experience.

We met the photographer first. He asked if he could play a song on Ben's guitar, then proceeded to perform "Blackbird."

Ben listened closely, then told him: "You know, you need to leave the high E open on that chord."

I groaned inwardly, wondering how the photographer might take Ben's Asperger's honesty and lack of social pretense. Fortunately, he really liked Ben and later told the reporter he was a "boy genius."

The day after the concert, Ben handled the phone interview like a pro.

"I first got into the Beatles in 1997," Ben told her. "When I first heard their songs, it was like their music spoke to me on a deeper level. Their music expressed revolution, rebellion and teenage energy, and I can relate to that."

Dave told the reporter: "Ben has musical gifts that I have never seen in any of my students. He hears something once and he knows it... We have an unorthodox teacher–student relationship—sometimes I feel I'm learning from him."

In the aftermath of the concert, we realized we needed to expand Ben's musical and social horizons further. Many times in the past, we had hoped to work with the school district to come up with a creative program addressing Ben's challenges through his strengths. But this time, as had been the case almost uniformly, the only way to create an appropriate program again involved a great deal of struggle and research and finally getting an attorney and going to mediation.

I had realized over the years that doing what was morally right to help develop my son's potential wouldn't win me any popularity contests. I had to be prepared to fight for his rights, to have people argue with me, at times dislike me, find me overly assertive.

As we were heading into mediation, our regional center counselor, Harry, came up with a brilliant idea which would lead us to the next stage of Ben's musical and personal education.

"We should have Guy design a program around music involving weekly recording sessions."

Energetic, visionary, Guy accepted the challenge. For the following year, accompanied by an aide, Ben was able to get a program involving hands-on experience, recording with Guy for two days a week and for two additional days with Guy's friend, Robert. Ben's program also included weekly phone sessions with Dave and bringing Dave down periodically for recording sessions.

People are astonished that Ben is able to do music lessons by phone (he picked up much of his keyboard knowledge relying almost solely on his auditory sense, which was also how he learned to read). When you focus on the strengths rather than just the challenges of an Asperger's person, you perceive many gifts that far surpass those of neurotypicals.

Ben quickly learned Guy's "language" (the Beatles) and Robert's (the Rolling Stones) and started recording the canon with each of them. With his remarkable acuity, he is able to quickly pick out the main melodic line, then each harmony, rhythm guitar, etc. Though he's never studied percussion, I was astonished one day to see him walk into Robert's studio and sit down at the drum set.

"Now I'm going to play Ringo's part in 'Help,'" he said, and proceeded to do so.

He quickly learned to multi-track each part for a recording. He also picked up recording technique and production in addition to performance.

This ability to handle performing as well as recording engineering characterized the late pianist, Glenn Gould, who it is now realized had Asperger's Syndrome. A gifted concert performer, Glenn Gould eventually stopped concretizing to concentrate almost exclusively on recording. His rendition of Bach's *Goldberg Variations* remains one of the greatest ever produced. I remember my pianist father's comment after hearing Gould perform in concert:

"He's a wonderful pianist," my father said, "though he has a tendency to hum along with the music."

Knowing now about Gould's Asperger's Syndrome, we can see his humming as a lack of concern over the social aspect of performing. Recording served as a perfect modality for him since humming could be edited out later.

Chapter Eleven

At the beginning of the following year, yet another door opened which would lead to radical changes in both Ben's life and my own. Ben's former respite supervisor came up with a suggestion.

"Have you ever considered having Ben move into his own apartment with a roommate?"

"Sure," I answered, "maybe in a couple years."

"What about in the next few months?"

Now I was truly astonished. "But how could he learn the necessary independent living skills so quickly?"

"What better way to learn than 'on the job,' in his own apartment?"

I felt like I was standing on the edge of a swimming pool, unsure of the water temperature. Yet even if the water felt cold initially, you could warm up after a few laps. As I've had to do at a number of junctures in my life, I answered:

"OK, how do we begin?"

"Paul, who's been working with Ben, has a lot of the qualities we need. He's intelligent, responsible, has a background in music. Have them start looking for an apartment."

They looked for a couple of weeks but weren't able to find the right place. Ben's former respite supervisor gave us a helpful tip:

"It's important to find a friendly building."

When a rare two-bedroom apartment came up in our own building, we had to make a decision in twenty-four hours.

"The building knows Ben and Ben knows the building," he pointed out.

So, not really knowing where this new road would lead us, we took the first step. Meanwhile, the renters who had occupied my grandmother's old house left and I had the possibility of moving into a larger space. I decided to overlap with Ben and Paul for a month during the transition.

As has often proven to be the case, Ben was able to adapt faster to a new situation than I anticipated. Except for one night when he knocked on my door, he began to adjust to his larger space and the following month, I moved into my grandmother's former house, feeling my physical space expand as my mental space had been doing for the past month by myself.

For the first time in almost 20 years, I could set my own hours, and arrange my own space and time as I saw fit. I still have continued to put in a tremendous amount of time and energy working on the many aspects of Ben's program—educational, musical, social, legal—including, most recently, taking over the direction of his supportive living program under a parent-directed pilot through our regional center.

The latest chapter in expanding Ben's world into wider and wider circles involves a remarkable educational institution called Musicians' Institute. As with many other resources, I found out about MI through Ben's teacher, Guy, who also teaches there.

"It's a school for kids who want to become rock musicians."

This time we were able to take the plunge more gradually, initially signing Ben up for a weekend workshop which he loved. Thanks to Harry at the regional center, who wrote a grant, Ben received funding for a week-long summer program which he enjoyed immensely.

"I feel I'm finally in the right environment where I'm appreciated as a musician, not just treated like a person with a disability," he said.

Again, proceeding on faith that Ben could be accepted into the year-long program, we were able to negotiate a mediation agreement that would enable him to attend. But when I spoke with the director, he said he wasn't sure Ben could benefit from the program. At this point, rather than seeing a brick wall and no way around, I needed to draw on all my resources of flexibility and the ability to find alternative routes. I also knew it was important to model these qualities, often difficult for an Asperger's person, for Ben.

Further discussions with the director uncovered valuable information—that he wanted the aide who accompanied Ben to play a more active role in the classroom. Guy also suggested I prepare on information sheet on Asperger's Syndrome and Ben's musical gifts for his instructors. For the first time since the second grade, Ben has been able to tolerate sitting in a classroom, often for two hours at a time.

The strength of his musical gift and interest has helped him overcome the challenge of his sensory oversensitivity. For the most part, Ben and his aide, Liu-ma, have been able to handle situations without my direct intervention. When I have needed to help problem-solve, I have tried to see myself as an interpreter in the widest sense of the word—trying to elucidate neurotypical culture for Ben, the Asperger's perspective for his instructors and the administrators. I can't stress strongly enough that parents should try not to take feedback defensively. Instead, they can view their roles as educators and interpreters who can understand and creatively bridge both perspectives. They can also model communication and flexibility skills to their Asperger's children.

Just as Ben's horizons have continued to expand in his new living situation, so have my own. In one very important area, spirituality, Ben led me to a door I might not otherwise have opened. Shortly after we moved into the ocean apartment, Ben embarked on a research project to collect every single photograph anyone had ever taken of him: no mean task covering at least two continents.

Concomitant with this project he started writing his autobiography, eventually totaling 150 pages, covering everything he remembered from ages one and a half to four, including entire conversations in both French and English. To my complete astonishment, Ben also remembers most of his dreams from a year and a half on.

"Doesn't everyone?" he's asked me.

"Not exactly," I've answered.

His first memory from age one and a half amazes me. He remembers me carrying him into the house and saying:

"On est dans la maison." ("We're in the house, we're home.")

"I remember wondering," Ben's told me, "why is Maman saying we're in the house since it's obvious where we are?"

As Ben searched out photos, his extreme Asperger's focus and determination sometimes overcame any thought of social politeness and practicality. I went along with his research project whenever I thought he had a reasonable chance of success, trying to coach him on asking politely. But one day he mentioned a friend of ours, a well-known artist.

"I don't have your photographic memory," I told him, "but I'm almost positive she never took a single photo of you."

But he was so determined I decided to call her myself, ostensibly to stay in touch after our move to LA.

"Please tell Ben hi," she said, "and I'm sorry I don't have any photos of him."

"I didn't think so," I said, then added, "but if you ever come to LA, be sure to look us up."

She laughed. "I will, but I rarely get down there," she paused. "But I do have a friend who lives in LA and I sense you'd have a lot in common." She described her friend, a writer and critic with whom I shared a number of interests.

A few weeks later, her friend and I got together in a café and talked about our respective life stories, and where our work and travels had taken us. As I described Ben's Asperger's Syndrome, the tortuous path which had led me back to LA, my separation, she said something totally unexpected.

"I know someone who might be able to help you. She's a world-class Jewish shaman, a highly spiritual person."

Her suggestion took me by complete surprise since I hadn't been aware I could even use any help from a spiritual direction. Though I had continued working with my therapist, Sue, by phone, as well as having occasional sessions with the dream therapist, exploring my religious tradition, Judaism, couldn't have been farther from my mind. If my relationship to Los Angeles had been ambivalent, my relationship to Judaism had been even more convoluted.

For one thing, I had never received a Jewish education, though our father had grown up in an Orthodox household.

"Music was Dad's religion," my sister says.

I'll never forget my father's reaction when I was nine and casually mentioned I'd told some kids at school I was Jewish.

"Never tell anyone you're Jewish," he said so firmly that for years, like a Spanish *converso*, I hid my Jewish identity.

Much later I learned that my father and his brother, as they were the only Jewish kids in their elementary school, had been beaten up.

My mother had received little Jewish education, coming from an extended family so assimilated they ate pork in Russia.

With little religious background, on the rare occasions when I did enter a synagogue, I experienced a similar discontinuity to what a Japanese Hawaiian friend described when she visited Japan:

"I looked like I belonged but I didn't act right. I walked like an American, not a Japanese woman, so people wondered what was wrong with me."

Though much of my life involves other languages and cultures, in a synagogue I felt shut out, an imposter, as if everyone else knew the prayers and music except me. I have a great deal of empathy for people with Asperger's Syndrome who often also look like they "belong" but are constantly crashing into invisible social walls they can't understand.

Having Ben led me to explore an area I might not have chosen to do without a child. Since I hadn't had a Jewish education, I was determined to give my child one. Greg, though raised a Lutheran, has always been very supportive of my own explorations of Judaism and was open to introducing Ben to this part of his heritage.

From pre-school on, I had Ben attend Sunday school. As at regular school, both his gifts and his challenges soon surfaced. He loved David who did music. One day, during a children's service, a small high voice broke into song in perfect pitch and with excellent Hebrew pronunciation.

As with learning to read in regular school, though Ben had appeared not to be paying attention, he had memorized much of the liturgical music. But also, as in his regular classes, he would walk out of the classroom when the mood struck him. So the synagogue Sunday school, around the same time as the regular one, no longer allowed him to attend.

During our year in Besançon, France, however, Ben and I joined the Centre Communautaire Juif (Jewish Community Center) and he made it through a year of French Jewish School (given on Wednesdays). I also was able to locate Jewish educational materials in French for children, which we took back to the US.

So, even when Ben was no longer welcome in either regular or religious school in the US, we began to celebrate Passover in French. We would invite French families, often French women friends married to American-Jewish men who wanted their children to become familiar with their Jewish background. Our French Seders helped reinforce Ben's bilingualism as well as giving him an opportunity for social contact.

One Passover, a few years before we left Ashland, the deeper meaning of the journey from bondage into freedom suddenly became clear to me on a very deep personal level. Suddenly, during our French Seder, I was struck by a parallel between my present situation and the Jews' imprisonment in Egypt. With no school accepting Ben, I had to add home-schooling to the already considerable load I bore of lay therapist, respite person, social skills interpreter etc. (not to mention parent). It took an immense amount of time and energy to research possible resources while having to deal with the mood swings of Asperger's Syndrome on a daily basis with very little help.

Ben, too, was in his own prison. A person with Asperger's Syndrome, without appropriate resources, lives in a prison of his own brain, lacking the key to unlock the gifts, to build bridges to the outside world. With few family support resources, the strains on our marriage were growing stronger as well. Asperger's parents need to realize that parents have different strengths and stress affects them differently.

But though I couldn't yet see any way out of my situation, the ancient story of Passover brought me hope. There *was* a journey from bondage into freedom. Somehow, I knew I would find the way. Just as we have to proceed on faith at the beginning in working to develop our child's potential, so do we need to leave the door of hope open. Parents also need to have hope that, further down the road, new strengths will emerge in them as well.

At this point, Ben recognizes his father's gifts and makes comments like:

"I inherited my love of linguistics and etymological dictionaries from my dad."

An English Ph.D., Greg has persisted in taking Ben to Shakespeare plays from an early age. A few years ago, Ben astonished us by quoting whole lines from *Macbeth*, again proving his and other Asperger's people's abilities to absorb information by unconventional routes.

The unconventional route, provided by Ben, that led me to the Jewish shaman brought me to a woman who could look at us and clearly see inside of what was going on spiritually as well as physically. My journey eventually took me to a synagogue dedicated to music and social justice. I was welcomed into the choir and sang for the High Holy Days. Because of space limitations, we had to sing each service twice so I received an immersion education in Judaism through music. Though not a person with Asperger's Syndrome, by working with one of my strengths, music, I was able to approach one of my challenges, lack of knowledge of Judaism.

THE AWAKENING OF Ben's musical potential brings to mind a science fiction story by Frederick Pohl, which I read as a child and has always remained with me. In "To See Another Mountain," an elderly scientist is confined in what appears to be a mental institution in an unknown mountain retreat. He has been constantly medicated with drugs, which cloud his memory but by focusing on a fragment of a childhood song, he begins to recall his past life. As details return to him, he starts to suspect that the supposed "therapy" has another purpose besides healing.

As his consciousness returns to him, he begins to understand he is a person of great potential and extraordinary gifts, including psychic ability. Rather than trying to treat him, frightened by the unusual nature of his gifts, his keepers have been trying to suppress them. Reawakening the consciousness of his potential is the first step to recovery and the continuation of his development.

From an adult perspective, I see this story of awakening untapped potential as a metaphor for Ben's life and my own. I hope that this focus on gifts and strengths as well as challenges may help other Asperger's families traverse the sometimes daunting but often rich imaginative landscape of their children's potential.

When we first moved to the ocean apartment, I found a note card with a quote about taking the risk to explore one's outermost limits. I immediately bought the card, not really looking at the picture until I returned home. Then I saw a woman wading into the ocean, her back turned from the land. On the back of the card I read: "Susan asks the question." Then the synchronicity of picture, quote and title struck me. Excitedly, I called the publisher.

"My name's Susan and I've just moved to the ocean."

I didn't elaborate on all the unresolved questions I was pondering.

"The artist has another picture," she told me, "called Susan Finds the Answer."

Extremely curious, I placed my order. When the second picture arrived, I saw Susan now standing sideways, equally balanced between ocean and land. I thought of sea boulders, rooted in land yet immersed periodically in water, maintaining their own solidity while being sculpted by the flowing powers of the ocean.

I sit in the ocean café, at journey's end, writing the last words of this narrative. I can't say where Ben's journey and my own will next take us, but may our explorations so far help other Asperger's families to perceive their own journeys as adventure and the catalyst for inner as well as outer growth.

Epilogue:
Empowering Parents

N ote: I encourage parents to "translate" the following suggestions into a language that fits your family.

Recognize your own strengths and gifts and share these with your children

In my case, these included foreign language and music. Other parents might be skilled in math, cooking, the sciences etc. Despite the challenges of raising a child with Asperger's Syndrome, you are not powerless and you have many strengths to give to your child including modeling how to advocate for his or her rights.

Be alert to recognizing and nurturing your Asperger's child's often extraordinary interests and gifts

Be open to searching out resources and specialists in the neurotypical community who may not have encountered people with Asperger's

Syndrome before. Often, specialized interest groups, say an automobile hobby club, will be delighted to welcome in an Asperger's kid whose depth of knowledge often exceeds their own. Our park horticulturist, for example, was happy to give Ben his own guided tour of maple species. Create more and more "cross-cultural experiences" where both the Asperger's person can benefit from having his or her gifts appreciated in a positive social context and the neurotypicals can benefit from the child's expertise.

Recognize that you, too, as well as your child, are on a positive journey of personal transformation

The skills you are learning, such as having to barter, and to research resources and agencies, will have unexpected benefits, such as occasionally meeting wonderful resource people who will inspire you just as you and your struggles for your child inspire them. These skills are also transferable to other areas of your life, teaching you how to differentiate between helpful and unhelpful criticism. You can't be afraid of criticism as you fight to create a strengths-based approach for your child. If you can be ready for criticism and accept it when valid, you'll be able to focus on what's really important—nurturing your child's genius.

Enjoy where your child's interests lead you

In our case, I never would have gone so deeply into exploring maps or the Smithsonian collection of Woody Guthrie recordings, to cite just a few examples.

Appreciate the spiritual dimension of the journey

At times, your child's unusual Asperger's perspective may go directly to the heart of many deeply spiritual and philosophical issues. Ben's question: "Where were our souls before we were born?" has led him to discussions with our rabbi, with Protestant and Catholic friends, as well as with a Tibetan Buddhist. The Tibetan Buddhist commented to me afterwards: "I can tell Ben's done a lot of reading in Tibetan Buddhism." "None at all," I replied, surprised. "Then how did he know three out of four of the fundamental laws?" Regardless of our own religious tradition and background, I feel it's important to be open to your child's spiritual interests and potential. Asperger's Syndrome children need to believe in their own future, that they were meant to be here to develop their potential and share their gifts with a larger humanity. Like all of us, they experience anxiety and a need to be loved as part of their driving forces.

Reach for the stars

By sharing your interest, enthusiasm, and strengths with your child rather than your anger and disappointment, you will be surprised at the level of sensitivity which emerges and how much your child really does understand what you're trying to do.

Prepare your child to live as independent a life as possible

Learning how to present as positive an appearance as possible on the outside, the child is more likely to have his or her inner gifts be appreciated. With an Asperger's person's disregard for social convention as well, often, as his or her inability to understand social interaction, this area can be one of the most challenging. The more the area to be worked on can be linked with one of the child's areas of interest, the greater the possibility of a "buy in." Recently, I came up with the heading: "Grooming Ben for a Career in Music" as a way to try to link physical appearance with his desire for a musical career.

Share your hopes and dreams for your child with him or her and listen to his or her hopes and dreams

Leave as many doors open as possible. Close only the doors of negativity while opening the doors of possibility leading to a career, love and possibly marriage, and even, one day, children.

Don't forget to take care of yourself

You need to stay in good shape physically, mentally, and emotionally to be the best advocate for your child. Try to spend part of every day nurturing yourself, be it through swimming, going to the gym, listening to music, or whatever.

Just being strong and surviving Asperger's Syndrome is not enough

During my years of struggle, sometimes I felt as though I was living in a snake pit, bitten by the venom of hate, anger, selfishness, envy, shame, and the trap of being governed by all of these feelings. Some of these snakes were power freaks. But by focusing on my child's positive potential and my own, I emerged from the snake pit, journeying from bondage into freedom. May this book inspire you and your child to do the same.

Sample Asperger's Syndrome Background Information to give to Teachers etc.

This information provides a model for presenting the positive side of Asperger's as well as the challenges; it summarizes some of the "life lessons" I've learned through raising Ben and which I hope can be useful to other parents.

- Asperger's Syndrome involves a unique combination of gifts and challenges.

- Well-known Asperger's individuals include Albert Einstein, pianist Glenn Gould, and composer Béla Bartók.

- People with Asperger's are often highly intelligent, musically or artistically gifted; this is coupled with a delay in social and emotional development related to autism.

- Though often very gifted and technically adept, they sometimes lack an understanding of appropriate social behavior and how to interpret emotions.

- Ben has absolute pitch, the ability to reproduce many musical styles including the Beatles and Bob Dylan, and a photographic memory. He's also bilingual in French and is teaching himself many other languages.

- His strong interest and ability in music can serve as a bridge into greater social understanding and peer relationships, and to entering a larger world through his music education.

- Ben will be attending class with an aide to help with transitions etc. Please feel free to talk with both of them.

- In addition, both Ben's roommate and his mother are more than happy to provide any additional information you might find helpful. [Supply contact information here.]